The Existential Lemonade Stand Essays

Joan Tornow

Library of Congress Control Number:2019908205

ISBN: 978-0-578-53248-6

Ink Lake Publishers
35003 5th Ave SW, Federal Way, WA 98023

John,
you are my sunshine

Contents

The Existential Lemonade Stand

It was a sweltering hot August afternoon, and I was driving my dog Toby to the walking trail for our daily outing. On days like this, the blacktop trail can be a bit warm for his paws, but he still insists on this daily routine.

So, we found ourselves driving down the street, a warm breeze flowing through the windows. Toby kept his head poking out into the hot afternoon sun, his eyes closed as if in rapture.

Suddenly my eye was caught by a young girl almost stepping into the street and wildly waving a hand-lettered sign.

Alarmed, I tapped the brake, but was relieved to see the girl was smiling. And as I read her sign, it all became clear: "Lemonade 4 Sale!" A few feet back, under the shade of a small tree, two other young girls were watching over a small refreshment stand.

I felt the pull of nostalgia, but promptly went through the mental calculus of whether to stop or not. I really didn't want lemonade right now. But – they undoubtedly needed the business. I didn't have my purse with me. But – there was money in the visor. I didn't have time. But – actually I did.

So, after lumbering over a speed bump, I pulled over to the curb and stopped. The young girl was sprinting toward me.

I extracted a couple of dollar bills from the visor and climbed out of my car, leaving Toby confused but with his window still open.

"I can take your order!" said the young salesperson. Her gaiety was something you truly don't see every day, and I had to admire her spunk. "You don't have to walk all the way back!" she explained. Apparently, she was prepared to be like one of those waitresses on roller skates who comes right up to your car. I remembered those from my youth, but that was a long time ago. Do they still do that?!

"That's okay" I said. We made our way back along the sidewalk toward the stand where her friends were eagerly awaiting our arrival. The girl who had flagged me down, let's call her the *chief entrepreneur,* seemed to be the one in charge. She walked along with her sign flapping under her elbow while rattling off the purchasing options: "We have pink lemonade, but also classic which is not pink but normal color. And you can choose small or large. We also have brownies and cookies!"

By now, we were at the stand where I was greeted with enthusiasm by the chief entrepreneur's business partners, the purveyors of three trays of baked goods and two tall pitchers of lemonade, both classic and pink. It looked pretty good!

"I'll take a small classic lemonade," I said, "And a brownie."

One of the girls poured lemonade into a paper cup while another picked up a brownie and placed it carefully on a napkin.

"That will be $1.00 total," said the chief entrepreneur.

I paid, but still had a dollar left over. And they all could see that I still had a dollar because, as noted earlier, I did not have a purse in which to tuck it.

"How much are the cookies?" I asked. I was pleased that they appeared to be homemade. It wasn't like their mothers had just bought them a couple bags of Oreos and told them to go play in the street. Which is what I usually encounter in these situations.

"Fifty cents each," said one, quickly adding, "I baked these, and Sharon baked the others." She pointed proudly to a tray of vanilla cookies and one of chocolate. They were displayed quite nicely on matching ceramic platters.

I chose one vanilla and one chocolate.

"Would you like me to wrap them up for you?" asked one, clearly pleased with her professionalism.

"That would be a good idea," I concurred. "I have my dog in the car, and I wouldn't want him to get into them. I would miss out on the cookies, and he would get sick!"

One girl grabbed a napkin and proceeded to wrap the cookies with great fanfare, the chief entrepreneur looking on with approval. Then, the chief entrepreneur said something that proved that she would succeed in our capitalist society: "If your dog dies from the cookies," she said, "I just want you to know that we also do funeral planning. Me and Heather planned a funeral for our friend's bird last week, and it was awesome. Everybody loved it!"

I laughed at that, sharing a bemused look with one of the girls who appeared to be worried about how I was taking this sales pitch. Truth be told, I was delighted. I picked up the baked goods with one hand while gripping the lemonade with the other. Then, purchases secured, I headed back toward the car where Toby was waiting with head hanging out the window, intensely interested in this unexpected delay.

Carefully walking over the speed bump en route to the driver's side door, I heard the chief entrepreneur's voice drifting toward me on a warm breeze. "Please tell all your friends about us. Especially if they have a bird!"

Ordering Cake

Recently I volunteered to order a cake for the writers group that meets every Wednesday at the Saltwater Unitarian Church. We had discovered last year that six of our ten members had birthdays in March. And so, this year we were to have our second annual birthday celebration. Last year we had enjoyed a delicious cake from our local grocery store. So again this year, I went there to order a cake.

It took a bit of time to snag someone's attention, as oven fans and store exhaust fans were creating a cacophony in this corner of the store. *They should have one of those bells that customers can ring to announce their presence*, I thought to myself.

Eventually a young woman responded, came out front, and asked how she could help. I told her I needed a cake – "this size" – as I pointed to a cake in the display case.

"Oh, quarter sheet," she said brightly.

"Yes," I confirmed.

She disappeared for a moment and returned with a form on a clipboard.

"What kind?" she asked.

"White cake with that raspberry filling if you still have it," I said. I was a bit concerned that she hadn't yet taken my name.

"We do have that filling," she said, scribbling rather furiously on her form.

"Your name?" she asked, suddenly rather officious it seemed. Well, probably she was overworked and trying to prepare some hot cross buns or something else on one of those steel tables way in the back where a hive of women with hair nets were tending to doughs, batters, and all manner of stainless steel cookware.

"Joan Tornow," I said. When she started on the last name, I quickly proceeded to spell it, as people always want to put a U after the T. Instead of an O.

"Could you repeat that?" she asked.

I spelled it again and looked to see if she had it. She had written 'TONY."

I said, "No, it's TORNOW."

She crossed out the name and tried again. I saw she had written "TONORY."

"I'm sorry," I said. "It's an unusual name. Let's try again."

As I spelled, she wrote, "TORNOWY."

"Just N-O-W" I corrected.

"I don't know why I want to put a Y in there, but it doesn't really matter," she said, "Because we go by the first name, anyway."

I saw she had written my first name as JONES.

"Unless it's important to you," she added, looking up from the clipboard. Her face was flushed and her eyes just a bit bloodshot. Had this poor woman been up all night in this hot, noisy kitchen?

Softly, I said, "Well, it is kind of important, actually. I'm sorry to be so OCD about this, but it has led to problems in the past." The truth of this could not be overstated. One example: When we moved to Washington State, it took us two years to get the local phone book to spell our name correctly, with the result that people trying to visit us during summer travels from our former home of Texas, could not locate us. That was, of course, before the Internet, or at least before Google.

This name-spelling issue had also come up countless times when we showed up for events only to be told our name was "not on the list." This always caused a few seconds of panic before we asked them to look our name up with the second letter of U. "Why don't you pronounce it 'Tornow' instead of "Turnow?'" some folks asked. Well, the Tornows have just always pronounced it that way. One theory is that they didn't want it to rhyme with "porno." More likely, it's just easier to say *Tur* than *Tor.*

The cake lady crossed out the name again and rewrote it. At risk of micromanaging, I leaned in a bit and peered at the form. A quick glance revealed that it seemed to be right. But, I couldn't help noticing that she had not written the name on the line marked 'Customer,' but a line or two below that. Oh, well. Close enough, I figured.

"So, what color?" she asked, quickly adding, "We just have spring colors now." She pointed to a huge apothecary jar filled with layers of sprinkles in four or five pastel shades. "That orange is nice," she said, pointing to a garish cake in the display case. I suppose that shade of orange could be considered a spring pastel, but should a cake resemble a traffic cone? The one next to it was a neon green that looked like it should be returned to the helmet of a Seattle Seahawks football player!

"Hmmm," I stalled. "None of those colors are quite what I had in mind."

"They really do want us to stick to the spring colors," she repeated.

"Well, what about chocolate then?" I asked, thinking surely *that* would be an option.

"Oh, of course," she said.

"Or white?" I asked. That had been my first choice but I had been afraid to ask.

"Sure!" she said. We proceeded to the words that would go on the cake – *Happy Birthday*, followed by a list of names. I had printed the names on an index card which I gave to her. She seemed grateful not to have to write down more names.

We then settled on the addition of a few flowers and maybe a shamrock or two, as it was March.

Next on the form was the pick up time. I said I needed it by 8:30 AM on Wednesday. She asked if 9:00 AM would be all right. "That would be cutting it really close," I said, adding that I had to be at the gathering by 9:30 AM.

"Okay, we can have it by 8:30 AM," she said. "I'll be here that morning, anyway, so I'll just do it myself by then."

As I signed the order form, she reassured me: "Don't worry about all the cross-outs. I'll be entering all this into our computer anyway. And, I'm clear on what you want."

I was grateful for her apparent concern and accommodation. "Thank you – Is it Chanda?" I asked, glancing at the name tag on her uniform. I pronounced it in a way that made it rhyme with "Rhonda."

She said, "Actually, it's Chanda. Short for Chandelier."

"Your name is Chandelier?" I asked.

"Yeah, my parents were sort of hippies, so I was named after a chandelier."

I pictured her parents toasting champagne under a chandelier as they fell in love. But, no, if they were hippies, I guess they would have been consuming something else under a chandelier. Something, let us say, more herbal.

Bringing my mind back to the present, I asked, "Did you get to see the chandelier you were named after?"

"Oh, they never had a chandelier," she explained. "They just liked light. My middle name is Aurora Borealis."

This conversation was quickly going down a rabbit hole. Had the cooks back there been smoking something contraband? It seemed entirely possible, what with all the fans, the midnight hours, and the general chaos. Had some smoke drifted perchance our way? I began to think differently about my grocery store!

"Well, they *were* hippies!" I concurred, struggling to get back to *terra firma.*

"Yes, they were," she said, as she pulled the form from the clipboard. Her bright eyes twinkled. She was just the sort of cheery person anyone would want to decorate their cake!

"What a great story and a great name!" I said. She smiled a happy smile.

As I walked away, I had a feeling that this had gone well, in fact better than expected. I felt all was right with the world: Ordering a birthday cake should be a joyful experience, and it was!

Two days later, I arrived at 8:30 AM to pick up the cake. Again, it took a bit of time to get someone's attention at the bakery counter. A woman came up and got my name. She went to the rack of cakes and I watched eagerly as she pulled out each of about ten cakes, examining the label of every single one. With a frown, she went back to the beginning and pulled them all out a second time.

She came back to me. "What was the name again?" she asked.

"Joan Tornow," I said, wondering if I should have said "Jones." I declined to spell Tornow, because I remembered Chanda saying they go by first names anyway.

The woman looked a third time, turned toward me, and shook her head.

My anxiety growing, I asked, "Is Chanda here?"

"No, she went home," she said.

At this point, a woman, perhaps a supervisor, who had been watching this scene unfold, emerged from behind a steel table and came up to the rack. She went right to a specific cake, pulled it out, and handed it to the original woman.

"Oh," said the woman, "Sorry about that. Here it is."

I looked through the cellophane and saw that it was, indeed, my cake, complete with white frosting, flowers, a few shamrocks, and the words *Happy Birthday*, along with six names, all nicely inscribed.

"Just pay at the front," she said with a perky smile.

I put the cake in my basket and headed toward the cashier stand at the front of the store.

Wondering what the problem had been, I looked at the computer-generated label affixed to the box. Under NAME OF CUSTOMER were the words "FANCY CAKE." Nowhere on the label did any part of my name appear. I figured the supervisor must have noted this anomaly earlier that morning, and that was why she was able to come to the rescue.

After paying for the cake and tucking it safely into the trunk of my car, I drove to the church. As I placed it on the table around which we gather, members of the writers group expressed their delight and soon erupted into song. Amid the merriment, we served up delicious slabs of cake on white saucers from the church kitchen.

So, all's well that ends well. I, Miss Fancy Cake, am grateful to Miss Chandelier Aurora Borealis for her efforts. I only hope that she left the grocery store that morning with a sense of accomplishment – not only from frosting our cake but no doubt a bunch of others. I hope her feet didn't hurt too much. And I hope she was headed for a place with gorgeous spring colors and an abundance of light.

Epilogue: A couple months after the episode described above, I again found myself in the bakery corner of my grocery store. I was browsing the tables of baked goods while looking for single servings of cake, available on occasion. Not finding this, I was happy to see one of the bakery employees bringing out some cartons of angel food cake. I asked, "Do you happen to have any individual servings of cake today?"

"I think we have some in the back, but just vanilla," she said.

I said, "That would be fine."

"They have chocolate frosting," she added. "Would that be all right?"

"Yes, that's perfect," I said. She looked familiar so I checked out her name tag. Could this be Chanda, short for Chandelier? But her name tag read "Chandra." Had I misread it on the earlier occasion?

Still convinced it was her, I said, "Oh, you're Chanda! You helped me with a cake one time. You decorated a birthday cake for our group!"

"Oh, good," she said. "Hope everyone liked it."

"Very much," I said. "But, I thought your name was Chanda, short for Chandelier. Not Chandra. Did they misspell your name tag?"

I assumed she would tell me that yes, the name tag is misspelled and that this happens all the time, much to her annoyance. Or, conversely, she would say that it's no big deal how people spell it. But instead, she said something that took me by surprise.

"You're right about my name," she said. "It's Chandra." She pronounced it *shanda*. Sensing my confusion, she explained, "The *r* is silent." After a pause, she added, "It's French."

Half-Caf at the Café

The line at my local coffee shop had stalled. The man in front of me had placed four tall travel mugs on the counter and asked for them to be filled "half with decaf."

The cashier asked, "And the other half?"

"Regular. Caffeinated," said the man.

The cashier proceeded to take two of the mugs and fill them from an urn behind her. "We'll have to do pour-overs for the decaf," she said brightly.

"Okay," said the man uncertainly. He then peered into the mugs and said, "But you only put coffee in half of these."

"Yes, you said you wanted half decaf," she said.

"No, all of them should be half-decaf," he responded. He seemed more distraught than the situation warranted. Although he wasn't exactly sweating, he looked like he should be.

"Oh, no problem," said the cashier. "I misunderstood you." She spoke with a perkiness that was just a bit excessive. Like someone on their first day at a new job.

She took the two mugs she had filled and emptied half of each into the sink. Returning to the counter, she took the other two mugs and half-filled them from the urn. "The decaf part will be in a pour-over," she said. "It will just take a few minutes." She then rang up the sale and gave him his receipt.

The mugs still sat on the counter, and it was not clear what he was to do. Perhaps he had noticed what I, too, had noticed. There had been no sign that she had put in an order for any pour-overs, so the transaction appeared to be stalled. The cashier looked a bit frazzled now, realizing that she couldn't ask for the next customer (me) because the man was not budging, and his four mugs were still sitting there.

"How long will the pour-overs take?" the man asked, now showing clear signs of exasperation. I suspect part of his frustration stemmed from her cavalier approach as well as the fact that all four mugs had their lids off, their steamy warmth escaping into the air.

"Oh, let me ask," she said. It took a few moments for her to flag down a barista who was rushing behind her, on her way to retrieve a breakfast sandwich from the microwave.

"How long will it take to get pour-overs for this customer?" she asked.

The barista paused long enough to view the four half-filled mugs sitting on the counter. When she looked puzzled, the cashier explained the state of affairs as best she could. The barista, in turn, glanced up at the man to get his take on the issue.

"I'm just wondering how long the pour-overs will take," said the man, "because this part's getting cold." He cast a nervous glance toward me and another couple of customers who had joined the line and were watching the scene with increasing interest.

The barista said, "Oh, we already have half-caf brewed. It's over here." She led the cashier to an urn a small distance from the other urns that held the caffeinated stuff.

I turned to exchange glances with the young man waiting in line behind me. We both rolled our eyes. These things happen at coffee shops all the time, especially, it seems, when one is in hurry. I was not in a terrific hurry this day, nor apparently was the man behind me. We were more bemused than annoyed. Surely the barista had misspoken and had meant to say decaf and not half-caf. How would this end? A veritable tempest in a teacup – er, travel mug!

The cashier took two of the travel mugs over to the newly-discovered urn and filled them, returning them triumphantly to the counter. She no doubt expected a smile from the customer, but instead he said, "Well, if you just added half-caf, doesn't that make them ¾ caf, and only ¼ decaf? I understood exactly what he was asking, as I had wondered the same thing. I had hoped he hadn't noticed, but he had.

The cashier said, "I just put in half-caf. Isn't that what you wanted?"

"I want half-caf," said the man. "But it was already half full of caf, and you added half-caf."

At this, the cashier looked totally at a loss. "I guess I don't understand what you want!"

The barista, eyeing the situation from nearby, now approached and asked, "What's the problem?"

The man explained that adding half-caf to a mug that already contained half a mug of caf results in ¾ caf. Clear enough to all of us who attended fifth grade. The guy behind me, and I, stifled chuckles.

The barista explained, "Oh, no, the urn over there is decaf." This contradicted her earlier pronouncement that it was half-caf.

What a difference a prefix makes! Again, I flashed back to fifth grade.

The man seemed mollified, and the cashier now proceeded to add the decaf to the remaining two mugs. She lined them up on the cramped counter, and the man transported them, two by two, to the counter hosting the cream, sugar, stir sticks, etc.

I ordered my short brewed coffee. Simple enough.

As the cashier turned her back momentarily to fill my cup from the urn, the guy behind me nodded toward the corner where the man was busily pouring additions into his travel mugs. "That guy still looks rattled," he said. "He's over there adding half and half to only half of his half-cafs!"

That totally cracked me up. Well, not totally. Only about half.

At the Library

As I drove up to the library, I saw that an emergency vehicle was parked there. Hesitating, in order to assess the situation, I watched as a couple of medics carried a man out of the library on a stretcher. The man was conscious and sitting up. He appeared to even be smiling, but was perhaps a bit dazed. I said to myself, "I want to read what he was reading!"

Blanks

My son Nick had recommended a book called *Blink: The Power of Thinking Without Thinking*. While my husband and I were awaiting our Thai noodles at a restaurant in Seattle, en route to the theater, I dashed out and looked for this at a bookstore we had just passed. I wouldn't normally abandon my husband at a restaurant to go shopping, but we were leaving for Mexico in two days, and I had to squeeze my book acquisitions in where I could. After all, Mexico was, for me, primarily a place to read.

I darted across the street, dodging the clouds of people making their way to The Seattle Center – people of all ages and dressed in anything from cut-offs to tuxedos, en route to comedy clubs, opera, or just the grocery store.

Entering the bookstore, a funky place which sold both new and used books, I didn't see anyone behind the counter. But as I made my way toward the rows of shelves, I spotted a guy sitting in cloistered seclusion back behind a huge computer monitor and stacks of books.

"Oh, may I help you?" he asked, as if awaking from sleep. He slowly stood up, eyeing me like an intruder.

"I'm looking for a book named *Blink*," I said.

"Do you know the author?"

"No, but I'll recognize it when I hear it. Can you look it up by title?"

17

He said he could and began typing into another computer that sat closer to the door where I'd entered.

"Hmmm," he said, pushing his knit cap back a bit on his head, a move that revealed a row of silver rings cupping one ear. "Yes, here it is – *Blank: The Value of Nothingness* by John Schirmer."

"No," I said "I'm looking for *Blink*."

"Oh, *Blink*!" he said.

After a few moments, he said, "Okay, here's a book called *Blink*, but it's pretty much the same thing – *Blink: The Power of Thinking Without Thinking* by Malcolm Gladwell."

I had to smile at his slacker attitude. He clearly felt that either book should suffice. No need to be picky: Blink, blank, what the hell difference does it make? They're both about nothing, after all.

I bought *Blink*, not *Blank*. But now I'm wondering if *Blank* might have been a better choice.

Off the Rails at a Brick and Mortar Store

Yesterday I went to Barnes and Noble, bringing with me my mocha from the adjoining Starbucks. Some might say this constituted a corporate morning, and point taken. But, I like the consistency of Starbucks drinks, and I try to do my part to keep brick and mortar bookstores alive and well. A leisurely visit to a bookstore is, for me, a "staycation," a mind-expanding and relaxing getaway.

Sinking into an easy chair, I set my mocha on the low table, along with the books and magazines I had snagged while making my way to this cozy corner. As I shoved aside the tumbling stack of books previously abandoned on the table, the titles caught my eye: *When Anger Hurts, The Anger Management Workbook, Anger Control Workbook,* and *Taking Charge of Anger.*

"Wow," I thought to myself. "Sure hope this person doesn't return in a rage at me for taking his/her seat!" I wondered where this person was now and whether any of these books had helped with the issue at hand. I decided to take notes on these titles for this essay, and worked my way down the stack. The last three titles were *The Dance of Anger, Loving Him Without Losing You, How to Get Your Lover Back,* and *Getting Back Together.*

Ahh. The story was coming into focus. The angry and hurt person was a woman, and her goal was to get her boyfriend, significant other, or spouse back.

19

With any luck, she had found some answers and solace in these books. Or, was she at this very moment collecting a new rash of books with titles like *Making Him Sorry, Getting Even*, or *Revenge: A Dish Best Served Cold*? I said a little prayer for her and hoped she had purchased something like *Be Yourself, Be Strong*. I don't know if there is such a book, but there should be! There's certainly a bounty of self-help books with this basic message. I know because I've resorted to bibliotherapy myself from time to time.

I leaned back in the easy chair and sipped on my mocha, grateful that I was feeling secure and happy on this particular morning. I was happily married and coping fairly well with the vicissitudes of life.

Humbled, I turned my attention to the books and magazines I had gathered to peruse. The first was *Gone Girl* by Gillian Flynn. After reading the first few pages, I knew this was a book I would buy. I then dipped into *Reason Magazine's* lead article: "Millennials Are Not Listening to You." This story had caught my attention because I thought it might help me understand a certain relative who, indeed, does not listen to me. He's not a millennial, but he is young and has certainly tuned me out.

A recent "conversation" with this young man went something like this: He: "Why are you telling me all about your trip?" Me: "Because you asked." He: "I asked if you had a good trip. I was looking for a *yes* or *no*." Me: "You don't get a simple *yes* or *no* from me. You should know that." He: [No comment] Me: "And, just for the record, when I ask you a question, I do *not* want just a *yes* or *no*." End of so-called conversation.

I sipped on my mocha, my drug of choice. And, turned to my next selection – a coffee table-type magazine called *Daphne's*

Diary. This British lifestyle magazine is full of Victorian illustrations, recipes, and cute little essays. Brain candy.

While perusing these, I couldn't help but overhear a loud nearby conversation between a bookseller and a customer. The bookseller was saying, "Oh, I know how you feel. The first time someone I knew died, I couldn't believe it. I was thinking, This is awful. This can't happen. But now I have a more philosophical view of death. What helped me was taking walks and just looking at … well, just looking at a tree, for example. You don't have to go out in the country. There are trees everywhere. Well, I'm just saying that helped me."

The customer responded in a barely audible voice and was even tearful. As the conversation progressed, it was clear that this bookseller was offering therapy for this woman. And, at the close, the bookseller said, "Well, come back and see me and let me know how you're doing. It will get easier, just hang in there."

So, brick and mortar stores can deliver therapy above and beyond the self help books, I concluded. Even my brief visit had lifted my spirits. On my way to the register to buy *Gone Girl*, a mocha-and-bookstore-high led me to grab a Little Golden Book from an end cap. This was a book for adults called, *Everything I Need to Know I Learned From A Little Golden Book* by Diane Muldrow.

As I flipped through the illustrations and catchphrases, I was delighted to see that iconic picture of Tootle the Train after he has left the tracks and is happily lollygagging in a lovely meadow. He has a loopy smile on his face, a daisy chain around his neck, and is surrounded by colorful butterflies. I think what young readers were supposed to learn from Tootle was that he, and everyone else, should stay on the tracks. But I'm pretty sure what stuck in our young minds was exactly what Muldrow, the author of this new book, had seized on: That *leaving* the tracks is actually quite rewarding! Indeed, Muldrow used this particular picture to illustrate the following advice: FROLIC. Indeed. Hear, hear!

At the Walking Trail

I was walking along the paved BPA Trail when I spotted a praying mantis sitting right in the middle of the trail. I stopped and stared. It was September which I guess is why the mantis had turned brown rather than green. Or perhaps they take on the color of their background which, in this case, was old blacktop.

Anyway, the mantis was just sitting there, hands folded in prayer. I took a leaf and coaxed the mantis onto it. Then, I took the leaf to the nearby grass and set it down. Without hesitation, the mantis moved to the grass and began walking away in that awkward way that mantises walk. I wonder if its prayers were answered.

Melody and Her Incredible Ego

A bunch of Americans and Germans were clustered in the crowded living room of a small house in Geilenkirchen, Germany. My husband John was an Air Force medic, stationed nearby, and I was a tagalong military wife. Melody, the wife of John's commander, was hosting a tea and pie social with the goal of strengthening ties between military personnel and local German residents. Because there was no base housing, we all lived off base in small rural towns.

Melody, along with her husband Russ, had planned this get-together several weeks earlier, but Russ had been unexpectedly deployed to another base for a few days. Melody, a seasoned military wife, was able to orchestrate this gathering just fine. A petite Southern belle from North Carolina, she was a gracious hostess. She used her bright blue eyes to good advantage, charming people with ease. Actually, she was quite the flirt, but she could get away with this, as people just laughed and chalked it up to her being from the South.

The room was so small that many of us were sitting on cushions on the floor, balancing our plates on our knees while finding just enough room on the small coffee table for our teacups. Melody was serving pecan pie that she had baked herself, using an old family recipe. And, she was serving strong British tea on Villeroy and Boch china teacups, manufactured nearby. The dollar was strong, and many military wives had splurged on this suddenly affordable luxury.

Although it was a chilly autumn evening, we were comfortable in the warmth of this home – feeling mellow from the hot tea, the pie, and the friendly conversation. The fact that we were an international group made us mindful that this was a somewhat formal occasion, so we strove to keep the conversation at an unusually elevated level. After all, most of us had read the official Air Force manual that provided guidelines for inter-acting with citizens of host countries. We were, for example, to avoid discussions of politics or religion.

Melody sashayed through the living room and kitchen, her skirts swishing, her dark hair falling this way and that as she leaned in to refill teacups or pick up empty plates. The stolid German guests blushed at times, perhaps just from the warmth of the room.

At one point, we found ourselves talking about food – a safe topic and a common denominator among people of all nation-alities. Melody brought up the topic of lobsters. With her story-telling prowess, she launched into an amusing story about the first time she had bought live lobsters, while they had been stationed in New England. "I was determined to cook up those lobsters the ways the locals did," she said, trailing a manicured finger along the side of her neck.

She swept her blue eyes around the room as if making sure she had everyone's attention before proceeding: "So first I had all those lobsters just a'crawling around in a bucket. But this one, it was climbing up on top of all the others. It was so aggressive and I thought to myself, that one's going to get loose!"

Melody had everyone's rapt attention as she continued: "I ran and got some oven mitts and grabbed that thing right around what I guess you'd call its stomach. Then I carried that crazy lobster to the bathtub. Russ was gone on night duty, so I had to do this all by myself!"

The military wives groaned with understanding. We often found ourselves taking on tasks which typically fell to husbands – rescuing cats from trees, changing tires, knocking down wasp nests. We'd all been there, although perhaps not with lobsters. But, back to the story.

"I was actually getting pretty scared," she said. "'Cause I was all alone, you know. Just me and this big thing that seemed to want to attack me." Her coy smile led us to wonder what would happen next.

"Well," she said, "Even after I had it in our little bathtub, it kept on waving those claws around and staring at me with those beady black eyes!" Everyone was chuckling, no doubt contemplating petite Melody transporting a gigantic writhing lobster from bucket to bathtub.

"I was so frightened," she continued. "I didn't know if it would stay in the bathtub. Before I went to bed,I checked on it, and it was trying to climb out. I didn't think it could escape, but I wasn't sure!"

Melody slid onto a bar stool and crossed one slender leg over the other. She continued: "So, finally I went to bed and pulled the covers up and just lay there, quivering. Like I said, Russ was going to be on duty at the hospital all night long." She was back in flirt mode. Along with avoiding topics like politics and religion, military wives should never, in formal social situations, talk about being in bed alone – especially not *quivering*. True, this isn't specified in the manual, but we all just know it instinctively.

Melody was about to finish her story with a coquettish flourish. Smiling at our upturned faces, she said, "I was afraid that lobster was going to crawl in bed with me!" Eyes dancing, she scanned the room to gauge the effect of this latest pronouncement. There was a notable pause as we all envisioned this dramatic turn in the story. An awkward silence prevailed. Melody awaited a response, but none came.

Finally, someone spoke. It was my husband, John. Taking a deep breath, he shook his head in disbelief and declared, "What an ego!"

Against a backdrop of quietly rattling teacups, everyone, including Melody, burst out laughing!

Their Appointed Rounds

I love the post office. I've even memorized their creed – literally etched in stone in the foyer of our current branch: "Neither snow, nor rain, nor heat, nor gloom of night can stay these couriers from the swift completion of their appointed rounds."

Okay, so I memorized this one day while standing in a long line on a rare occasion when I forgot to bring something to read. It was hard to memorize till I unlocked the secret pattern. Snow, rain, heat, gloom of night. That seems to take us through the year – starting with January's snow and ending with December's gloom of night, with the rain of spring and the heat of summer sandwiched between.

After that, it's mostly a matter of remembering the adjectives which are sparse and not necessarily where expected. For example, the couriers don't get an adjective, although I'm always tempted to say they are brave or heroic or loyal. In the official creed, though, they're just couriers. But their completion – that is *swift*, and their rounds – *appointed*. A nice ring to that – *appointed rounds*.

But I digress. Aside from this poetic motto, why fall in love with a post office?

Well, the post office is a place where people gather, albeit to send letters and packages to people elsewhere. Still, there seems to be a certain camaraderie – a sense that we're all in this together. And, we all pretty much know the ropes.

While many complain about rising postage costs, I still think that 62 cents is a small price to pay for transporting small pieces of paper from, let's say, a house on the west coast to, let's say, another house on the east coast. Rather remarkable when you think about it. Oh, sure, letters are occasionally shredded, lost, or mis-delivered, but they generally arrive promptly and in good shape. The package delivery system is also a bargain. Yes, packages sometimes take a circuitous route and arrive a bit bruised, the brownies inside stale and crumbling. But by and large the system works pretty well.

I also like to gaze at the weathered faces of the clerks. Many of them look like they've spent years tromping across Alaska in worn snowshoes. I like to think that during their courier years, they paid their dues, faithfully carrying our precious cargo through snow, rain, heat, and gloom of night. Now, in their golden years, they've been rewarded with a less challenging job, serving at the counter. I watch one of them pull out an album of pictorial stamps and discuss them with a customer. "Well, if you want colorful, you could go with the Janis Joplin," she says. "But, if that's not your thing, this one on Frank Lloyd Wright is kind of nice." I watch with veneration from my distant location in the line.

I suspect there are customers who don't share my exalted view of the post office and its workers. Yes, we could all communicate by phone or email. And, if we must send letters, we could at least purchase our stamps online. But going to the post office is a ritual some of us are loath to give up. It is perhaps a remnant of that ancient rite of going to the town center to conduct one's business. With so many of us living in sprawling suburbs with no town center, the post office suffices. Once I even saw the mayor at the post office. No doubt he could have had one of his assistants run this errand, but perhaps he likes going to the post office as much as I do. (Or, was he just checking to see if any of his new hires were depicted on the Most Wanted posters?)

Yes, despite all the changes in recent years, the post office stands its sacred ground – even as it dispenses its fleets of trucks and mail carriers to deliver the mail right to our doorsteps. I have yet to see commemorative stamps featuring postal workers, although such stamps were apparently released for a short time back in 1973.

Meanwhile, inching forward toward my turn at the counter, I silently pay homage to the postal couriers who, over the years, and unencumbered by a single adjective, have valiantly trudged on through the snow, rain, heat, and gloom of night – for us – to *swiftly* complete their *appointed* rounds.

A Boy On a Scooter

There's a walking trail where I often take my dog for an afternoon stroll. I park my car in a cul de sac near the trail, and over the years, I've become acquainted with some of the children who play in the street there.

Recently, as I was returning to the car, I spotted a little boy on a scooter racing toward Toby and me. I paused so we could say Hello. He said, "I know your dog! That's Toby, isn't it?"

"Yes," I said. "You have a good memory!"

He was now patting Toby who was wagging his tail enthusiastically. Toby loves this kind of attention, especially from children.

Gazing up at me, the boy may have noticed that I look like a grandmother. He said, "My grandma is coming to visit next week."

"Oh," I said. "That's wonderful! Where does she live?"

Without so much as a pause, he said, "At the end of a very long driveway."

With that, he said, "See you later, Toby!" and wheeled back down the street.

Dissonance, Salsa, and a Brown Eyed Girl

My husband and I, vacationing in Los Cabos, Mexico, had just settled down at a table in a restaurant overlooking the harbor. After ordering Pacificos – a local beer – I asked the host if this restaurant makes salsa at tableside.

"*Si, si, amigos,*" he said. He immediately summoned a young man in a chef apron and hat who wheeled up to our table a cart on which he had the makings for salsa – freshly roasted tomatoes and tomatillos along with little dishes of chopped jalapeños, oregano, cilantro, and onion.

"*Caliente?*" he asked as he dumped two plump roasted tomatoes into a mortar bowl made of volcanic rock.

"Mild," I said, watching him deftly slice the tomatoes into quarters with a knife before picking up the pestle and vigorously crushing the tomato pulp against the rough craggy inside of the mortar.

Tomatoes crushed, he added the tomatillos and muddled them as well. He then began to empty the bowls of spices into the mix, pausing when he got to the chopped jalapeño. He held out a teaspoon of the stuff and asked, "*Como este?*"

"*Mas!*" I said. Yes, my stomach dictated mild, but my taste buds still craved spicy hot.

Soon we were dipping thin hot corn chips into this warm and unbelievably flavorful salsa. Heaven!

And heaven, as if to put frosting on the cake, added one more ingredient: From the patio restaurant next door, just over the railing from where we sat, came the strains of Van Morrison's "Brown Eyed Girl."

Hey where did we go?
Days when the rains came
Down in the hollow
Playin' a new game
Laughing and a running hey, hey
Skipping and a jumping
In the misty morning fog with
Our hearts a thumpin' and you
My brown eyed girl
You, my brown eyed girl

I felt the spirit of the 60s surge through me, and my sandaled feet began to tap to the beat on the worn wooden floor.

Just then, two musicians approached our table, one with a guitar, the other with a mandolin. The guitar player began to gently pluck the strings, playing along to the strains of "Brown Eyed Girl" that already filled this space with music. His playing added a stereo dimension with a decidedly Mexican flavor – you know, the little ornamentations and extra notes. Think Mozart on margaritas.

The musician saw my smile and asked if we'd like him to play something. Struggling to communicate, I said something like, "*Puede cantar Brown Eyed Girl con este y entonces otra vez?*"

"*Si! Si, si, si,*" he responded. Grinning, he added, "*Por supuesto.*" Yes, of course.

I somewhat smugly concluded I had gotten my request across: Can you play "Brown Eyed Girl" along with the music playing and then play it again, starting at the beginning of the song? I figured the Van Morrison piece was more than half over and that this street musician would not mind playing it one and a half times. His "*Si, si, si*" led me to believe we were on the same wave length.

But, to my dismay, the two musicians began playing the song from the beginning! Since the recorded version could still be heard loudly, and was halfway through, there was now a disturbing cacophony.

It sounded something like this:

Hey, where did we go?
Days when the rains came
Laughing and a running hey, hey
Going down the old mine
With a transistor radio
All along the waterfall, with you
My brown-eyed girl
Do you remember when we used to sing
Sha la la la la la la la la la la te da
Standing in the sunlight laughing
Hiding behind a rainbow's wall
Whatever happened
Slipping and sliding
Just like that
Sha la la la la la la la la la la te da, la te da
Skipping and a jumping
In the misty morning fog with
Our hearts a thumpin' and you
My brown eyed girl

You, my brown eyed girl
So hard to find my way

Now that I'm all on my own
Sometimes I'm overcome thinking 'bout
Making love in the green grass
Behind the stadium with you
My brown eyed girl

My mind reeled. One second I was hiding behind a rainbow, then I was making love in the green grass, only to find myself in a waterfall singing *Sha la la la la la la la la la la te da!* Then I was slipping and sliding in a stadium with a transistor radio and going down into an old mine with my heart thumping. Good Lord, was this a love song or some sort of terrible nightmare?!

It was somewhat of a relief when all this brown-eyed girl stuff came to an end. John paid the musicians, we thanked them, and they wandered off.

Sheesh! Now that it was relatively quiet, the waiter came and took our order for chicken fajitas. Sipping our Pacificos, we gazed out at the boats rocking gently in the water which now reflected the blush of the sunset.

A few strains of music drifted back into my mind:

Laughing and a running hey, hey
Skipping and a jumping
In the misty morning fog with
Our hearts a thumpin' and you
My brown eyed girl

I felt like the brown eyed girl with my brown eyed boy – together in an enchanting evening glow, secure in the knowledge that tomorrow we two would sip coffee from our balcony and, hearts still a thumpin,' would revel in the misty morning fog.

Morrison's "Brown Eyed Girl," despite its jaunty melody and mostly joyous images, is actually about a couple that broke up. Yet John and I are still together. It's been over forty years since we met and rode our bikes to the ice cream store. And walked together under the cherry blossoms. And rode across the country in a forest green VW.

And here we were, relaxing in a restaurant in Los Cabos, our eyes dancing as our feet touched under the table. A deep red salsa of roasted tomatoes and tomatillos warmed our tongues.

We've certainly had our days of dissonance, days when the rain came. It hasn't been all rainbows. But delicious moments of contentment come unbidden – like this moment with this music and this food.

*****

After we ate, we wandered along the harbor, gazing at the sparkling water. We smiled at the names painted on the anchored boats: *Just a Splash, Present Perfect, Querencia, SS Recess,* and *This End Up.*

We caught a taxi back to our hotel and, after paying the driver, we wobbled over the cobblestones to the hotel lobby. Inside, we said "*Buenas noches*" to the lone but smiling clerk behind the counter and walked through to the back exit, glass doors that slid open to the quiet gardens and pools between the hotel and the ocean. As always, we paused at the flamingo enclosure to pay our regards to the half dozen stately birds that high-stepped cautiously inside their oasis of grass and ponds. Even in the gathering darkness, their bright pink surprised us, as always.

Ambling toward the ocean, we shed our sandals, depositing them at the top of the steps going down to the beach. Then, we walked along the sand – still warm from the day's sun. We saw, out past the breaking waves, the twinkling lights of the resting fishing boats.

The colors of the sunset had faded from the sky, leaving just a band of silver at the horizon.

I reached out for the hand of my brown-eyed boy, and he reached for mine. I could still hear the music, and I trusted he could, too: *Sha la la la la la la la la la la la la ti da!*

I'd Like to Lay My Burdens Down – But Where?!

What a nice feeling to walk into a house or office and find an empty hook for one's coat, and a nearby shelf for one's purse or briefcase, along with various bundles. And maybe even a place, on rainy days, for a dripping wet umbrella. But many times we find no such amenities. We're left to improvise, awkwardly juggling things or balancing them on our laps.

Growing up in a chaotic household where hooks and shelves were either rare, or already over-capacity, I didn't give these conveniences much thought. But, later, I realized how important hooks and shelves can be – not only because they simplify life, but because they convey in some subtle way that each person belongs and that his or her needs have been anticipated and provided for. My childhood family certainly meant well, but as a middle child of parents with attention deficit disorders, life was, as I said, chaotic.

I discovered the importance of hooks and shelves during my first days of college. Feeling lost and insecure when I arrived at my spartan dorm room, I immediately began unloading my stuff onto the strategically placed hooks and shelves. These conveniences seemed to say, "Okay! We were expecting you!" And, there is hardly any space more in need of hooks and shelves than a tiny dorm room in which two adolescents must struggle to stay organized.

Since my college days, I've grown increasingly appreciative of hooks and shelves. While relatively insignificant in the scheme of things, hooks and shelves don't just simplify life. They acknowledge our shared humanity – the simple everyday needs we have in common.

I personally breathe a sigh of appreciation when I arrive at a destination and find, in addition to an empty chair, a hook for my coat and maybe even a little table on which to rest my purse, my book, my cell phone, and often, it seems, a sheaf of papers relevant to an imminent activity or conversation.

By the same token, I am puzzled by what is often a total lack of these essentials – especially in an office – where dozens of people arrive on any given day and face the universal, and truly predictable, dilemma of where to put one's stuff.

Take my primary care doctor's office suite, for example. Upon being called from the waiting room, I am guided down a narrow carpeted hallway toward one of the gleaming sterile exam rooms glimpsed in the distance. Suddenly the nurse stops and gestures toward a scale nestled in an alcove. "Please step on the scale," she says. As I do so, I am intensely aware of the added weight I am carrying – my purse, book, and heavy coat. There is no hook, no shelf. I sometimes put these items on the floor, but this is an unsatisfactory solution. The floor is covered with old frayed and stained carpeting – certainly not subject to the daily scrub-down given the examining rooms. I know about that because one of my college jobs consisted of scrubbing exam rooms, and scant attention was ever given to the hallways, especially if they were carpeted.

I generally try to enlist the sympathy, or at least interest, of the nurse when I say, "Hmm – I should put these down, right?" – appealing to her sense that the weight should be of the person's body, not of the person and all the clothing and accoutrements present. I can envision a scenario in which the doctor notes a weight gain that, in reality, simply reflects that the patient happened to be wearing, that day, a heavy coat and knee-high winter boots. And, perhaps at the previous appointment, the patient carried a slim volume of poetry but today is toting a hefty copy of *War and Peace* – the big print edition! These factors surely affect one's stats! Why even bother weighing someone when all of this goes unaccounted for?

I sometimes point to a place on the wall and say, "They should put a couple of hooks right here, don't you think? And maybe a shelf?" The nurse, bless her, seems to share my consternation. But I nevertheless get the impression that she has no real interest in solving the problem.

After I have been weighed, and my height noted from the vertical ruler, I'm led to the exam room where I'm directed to sit down. At least, here I can drape my coat and purse over the back of the plastic chair. I have to get creative if I have a book and umbrella, especially if I'm directed to roll up my sleeve for the blood pressure cuff. Am I the only one, or do almost all patients wrestle with such logistics every single time they go to the doctor?

Once I even mentioned to the doctor – the one I've been seeing for ten years now – that it would be nice if they could put some hooks near the scale in the hall. He chuckled in agreement, rolling his eyes a bit, as if I had said, "Wouldn't it be nice if they could prevent rain in Seattle." I mean, the solution I'm proposing is actually *doable* – not something magical we can all only dream about!

Recently, I went to have my teeth cleaned at an upscale perio-dontist office. When I entered the treatment room, the hygienist directed me to put my purse on a nearby counter. This counter, as it so happens, is quite close to the counter where the dental tools are lined up in their racks. While I was grateful for a place to put my purse, I hesitated and asked, "Here?!" As I stalled for time, I remembered the recent TV report on how the bottoms of women's purses are teeming with bacteria, due to being constantly placed on floors, including the floors of bathroom stalls.

The hygienist insisted, in a friendly way, that I put my purse on this counter. So, I did so, but not happily. I'm not a germophobe, but I do believe in common sense. Hooks and shelves can be good for our health.

But, to return to more pleasant visuals, consider what it's like to enter a thoughtfully appointed hotel suite. As the door closes behind you, you find yourself in a well-scrubbed tiled hallway, replete with hooks and shelves. Here, you hang up coat, keys, camera, binoculars, tote bag, and so forth. A small alcove is fitted with low metal shelves for shoes or boots.

Wheeling your suitcase a bit further, you see a strategically-placed luggage rack. Nearby, an open closet reveals a collection of hangers, including clip hangers for slacks, padded hangers for dresses, and plenty of regular hangers for all the other clothes you've brought. Hooks on the side sit at the ready for belts and scarves. A built-in ironing board can be folded down, and a small steam iron sits right there on its own little shelf!

Walking into the bathroom, you note shelves near the sink where you can place your makeup bag without having to cram it into a corner of the counter, behind the soap dish, where it is bound to get wet or even to topple right into a sink-full of water.

A phone charging station is placed on the desk, and another one on a bedside table, such that you can charge your phone while sleeping, and still be able to turn off the alarm without having to leap out of bed and trip on, well, a tote bag that had no home of its own. When you wake up in the morning, you can easily locate all your things, predictably stored near where you will be using them. A hotel suite like this eases the hassles of travel and lets you focus on whatever is happening in your life, whatever brought you away from home in the first place.

As we travel through life, we find ourselves in a variety of situations and places. Sometimes the circumstances are happy, sometimes not so much. Often we arrive at places with at least some degree of trepidation or uncertainty. We may be outsiders or newcomers. We may be sick or grieving. We may be seeking employment or even food or shelter. We may be just a bit lost or confused. Hooks and shelves, when thoughtfully placed, acknowledge our journey. Though they are not human, they are extensions of the spirit and affirm our humanity. Meeting us exactly where we are, they offer a little help. They seem to say, "Welcome! We were expecting you! Take a load off."

A Katrina Flood Re-Enactment

It had been awhile since I had jogged on the Saghalie track, about a five-minute drive from our house in a suburb of Seattle. It was one of the last days of summer, a Saturday in 2006, and I felt like a run. There wouldn't be many more nice evenings like this one, as the autumn rains would soon be upon us. Today, the sun had been shining from early morning until the current dusk, and I savored its warmth.

The Saghalie Middle School track, co-owned by the public schools and the park system, is behind the school and has its own parking lot. As I approached the path curving past the basketball courts, the tennis courts, and the volleyball courts, I noticed that the path was not its usual chalky gray but instead a shiny-black. The pavement was wet – really wet, as in rain-slicked. How could that be, I wondered, as it hadn't rained in at least a week. Yes, the sun threw long shadows at this time of year, but it still cast a lot of heat, too.

As I drew closer, I saw that the path was indeed wet – almost a river, with water spilling along it and gurgling into storm sewers. The cause of all this water was that the couple dozen sprinkler heads on the nearby hillock were on, throwing water up and about with mechanical gusto. The grassy knoll near the volleyball court was so wet that water was pouring from it in flash-flood mode. The lawn had clearly absorbed all it could. And as for the volleyball court itself, the sand was dark with water. Indeed, three middle-schoolers were having a grand time building dams and sluices, talking with great excitement.

These sprinklers must have been going full bore since yesterday, Friday. What a waste of water and money! The school budget literally going down the drain. For the next 40 minutes, I jogged and walked around the track, stopping for a while to do sit-ups on the bleachers. By this time, the dozen or so other walkers had headed home. It was getting darker, and the autumn breeze, picking up at nightfall, felt chilly.

Heading back toward my car, I encountered a river of water pouring downhill along the path. The sprinkler heads punctuated the quiet with their rhythmic spinning, still fanning their water into the air with abandon. It was impossible to cross the resulting river without getting my feet, and even my socks, wet. With soggy shoes, I proceeded to where the boys were still playing with the wet sand, and I stopped to chat. "Is the sprinkler broken?" I asked.

"No," said one. "It's just on."

"I wonder if we could turn it off," I suggested.

"No, you have to have a special key," said another.

After pausing to digest this information, I asked, "So you tried to turn it off?"

"No, we can't," said the third boy. "I bet the sprinkler guy is going to really be in trouble."

"Is this your school?" I asked. I was already planning to phone the fire department when I got home. Civic duty and all that.

"Yes, we all go to school here," they said with apparent pride. "The sprinkler guy is never here on the weekends, though."

The boys continued their work, piling wet sand into makeshift dunes. Changing gears, I asked, "What are you building?"

"This is New Orleans," said one, gesturing to a veritable city of sand, complete with a levee built around it. "Right after the hurricane," he added.

"When the levees broke after Katrina," he pointed to a breech in one wall, "All the water went down here." He pointed to where he and his friends had placed clumps of sand in a big ring on the grass, circling a sort of lake that had clearly resulted from the nonstop sprinklers.

"Wow, how did you know about Katrina and the levees?" I asked.

"We studied it in school."

"Oh, that's great!" I said. And really, it was great. Hurricane Katrina had struck New Orleans a little over a year ago, but these boys had studied it in school and still remembered the key elements in the catastrophe in which almost 2,000 people had died. It was gratifying to hear that their teacher had used this disaster as a teachable moment. I wondered if these students also knew that hundreds of people were stranded in the Superdome for days without food, water, or adequate plumbing in the bathrooms.

I wondered also if their teacher had taught them about the government incompetence, the gross failings of local officials and of FEMA. Had teachers discussed the diaspora of the city's poor who had been flung out across the country and wrongly labeled "refugees" instead of displaced persons? I wonder if they heard that Barbara Bush, on visiting a Houston relocation site, had said, "And so many of the people in the arena here, you know, were underprivileged anyway, so this is working very well for them." It would be hard to fit all this into *ad hoc* curriculum, given all that must be "covered" in school.

Had they learned that government officials had passed the buck, hiding behind the refrain, "That's not my job" – even, apparently, when it was? In particular, Mayor Ray Nagin, Louisiana Governor Kathleen Blanco, and President George W. Bush, had all tragically failed to take the steps needed to mitigate this disaster. And the head of FEMA, Michael D. Brown, was rightfully blamed for a colossal failure to take timely action to warn those in harm's way.

Brown had also failed to provide for hundreds of survivors left homeless and hungry after the storm had passed and the levees had broken, causing deadly flooding. Despite the clear negligence of Michael Brown, President Bush publicly lauded him with the notorious comment, "You're doing a heckuva job, Brownie."

And now, here were these boys, knowing that sprinkler guy is going to get in trouble for leaving the sprinklers on, but also convinced that they themselves are helpless to affect the situation. That no one has any power to address this but sprinkler guy.

As I walked on, there was a part of me that wanted to go back and lecture them, tell them that they should always think what they can do to solve a problem – even if they didn't cause it, even if it's not their job. They did see the problem, so they should at least give some thought to addressing it. But I just walked on.

At home, I went to my computer and looked up the phone number for the fire department of our city of Federal Way. I was pretty sure someone there would know how to turn off the water supply for these sprinklers. Of course, I wasn't going to dial 911. I wasn't going to cause a dozen firemen to jump into their boots and go careening down the streets on a gas-guzzling truck, siren wailing. No, that would be overkill. But surely they must have a non-emergency line.

A Google search got me the phone number of the fire station closest to us, and I phoned there. A voice said, "You have reached the Federal Way Fire Department. Please listen to all options. We value your call. If this is an emergency, please hang up and dial 911. If you are calling to get information about fire prevention, inspections, permits, or plan review, please press 1. If you are calling the administrative office, please press 2. If you want to hear general information about job opportunities, CPR, first aid classes, recreational burning, or fireworks, press 3. If you want more options or numbers for other fire stations, press 4. To hear this menu again, press 5."

I hung up and racked my brain for the name of our water utility company. Lakehaven! That's it. Their website listed their numbers as follows: Emergency After-hours (253) 941-1516; Main Number (253) 941-1516. Same number. Without much hope, I dialed that number and heard the following:

"You have reached Lakehaven Water Utility. We are closed now. Our hours are Monday through Friday, 8 AM till 5 PM. If you are calling about a water or sewer emergency press 1." [a loud beep as I pressed 1.] Then, "If you are calling for a water emergency, press 1. If you are calling about a sewer emergency, press 2. If you want to hear these options again, press 3." [I pressed 1.] "If your water has been shut off due to nonpayment, you must make your payment at the office between 8 AM and 5 PM, Monday through Friday to reinstate your water. If you have a water emergency, press 5." [I pressed 5.] "If your water has been shut off due to nonpayment, you must make your payment at the office between 8 AM and 5 PM, Monday through Friday to reinstate your water. Please press 2 for further inquiries about your account. If you have a water emergency, press 5. If you have a sewer emergency, press 6."

I pressed 2 and when the recorded voice asked for my account number, I quickly mentioned Saghalie and the flood behind the school before the beep notified me my time was up. I hung up with growing frustration. How could I recommend this sort of citizen action to those boys? Maybe they were right. No one but sprinkler guy could fix this, and he wouldn't be in till Monday. And then, yes, he'll fix it, and why should anyone care if he's in trouble? Or, if a lake's worth of potable water has just gurgled down the storm sewer? There was a number listed for the administrative offices, so I called there and left a message.

What could I try next? Maybe the Federal Way Schools? I looked at their website, but there was no immediate path to what I was looking for, so I clicked on "departments." Scanning the alphabetical list, I came to "maintenance." There was the name of one person, let's call him Jim Brown, along with two phone numbers for him, the second one asterisked. I remembered the little boy at the track, saying, "Whoever's job it is is going to be in trouble." Surely, this Jim would want to stop in its tracks a sprinkler system gone wild. Even if he wasn't sprinkler guy, sprinkler guy probably worked for him.

With the hunch that the asterisked number might be a cell phone, I dialed it. No, it wasn't Jim Brown's cell phone, but the message I got provided his cell phone number. Hot on the trail of the head of maintenance, I dialed the asterisked number again, this time with a pen in hand to jot down the cell phone number provided. And then I dialed *that* number, and lo and behold, I got a real human being: Jim Brown, head of maintenance for the Federal Way Schools.

I gave Jim Brown my name and briefly described what I had seen behind Saghalie Middle School. "How did you get my number?" he asked, suspiciously. I told him I had tried the fire department and water department first, but then got his number from the Federal Way Schools website. "Hmm," he said "I'm going to have to do something about that."

"I'm sorry to be disturbing you on a weekend," I said, "but I thought you'd want to know. Those sprinklers have probably been on for 48 hours already, and by Monday, it will have been 72 hours or more."

"Are you suggesting that they were on Friday, when school was in session?"

"Well, maybe not, but I've seen them running on Friday mornings, so certainly they may have been on for over 24 hours."

"What were you doing there? Are you on the school staff?"

Now I was getting annoyed. "No, I run on the track there. It's a community resource, you know. I'm just trying to report a problem, as a citizen," I said. "I know the schools are strapped for funds, and I just hate to see all that water, and money, going down the drain."

"Well, you should have gone to the listing for 'security' on our website."

"I didn't see that," I said. Why was this conversation all about phone numbers and not at all about sprinklers? With Jim still on the line, I clicked back to the department's home page. In a list of about 100 departments, stretching down the left side of the screen, there was the tiny word, security, and I pressed that. I had to scroll down for several seconds before finding a phone number – a number followed by the words, "Monday through Friday, 8 AM till 4 PM."

"There's no off-hours number for security," I said.

"Well," he replied, "You could have found an emergency number on the front door of the school."

I was now doing not so much of a slow burn as a quick fry. I was pretty sure this wasn't sprinkler guy, nor did he seem to care much about sprinklers, water, or budgets. "So, you're not really interested in sprinklers that have run amuck at one of your schools?" I briefly contemplated the sprinklers running for one more day and two more nights before sprinkler guy would show up, slam his hand on his forehead, and mutter some expletive before using his magic key to shut the things off.

But this guy, head of maintenance, seemed not the least bit concerned. It was all I could do not to say, "You're doing a heckuva job, Brownie!" Maybe I should just phone Sean Penn! He had taken matters into his own hands after Katrina, flying down to New Orleans and going out in a rowboat to help rescue people.

By now I was sure that the beeping I was hearing was call waiting, maybe the fire department or the water department. "I have an important call waiting. I have to go," I said and abruptly ended this dead-end conversation. Perhaps Jim was left scratching his head and saying, "Which school did she say that was?" Or, perhaps muttering, "Note to self: Get phone number taken off district website."

The call waiting was, indeed, someone from the Lakehaven Water Department. Someone had listened to my voicemail! An official there thanked me for my interest, got some more information, and said he would head to the school right away.

The next morning, I drove to the track, curious to see if the sprinklers had been turned off. There were no cars in the lot, but there was an official-looking pick-up truck pulling away. I jumped out of my car and flagged him down. "Were you checking on the sprinklers?" I asked.

"Yes," he said.

"I'm the one who phoned about it yesterday. I just wondered, for future reference, who I should call if I notice something like that again."

"Just call us again. We really appreciate that. I came over last night and shut everything off. I just came back today to make sure the timer hadn't turned anything back on. And to check on the drainage. Everything looks good now." He smiled and prepared to drive away.

I walked over to the saturated sand, the soggy remains of New Orleans now abandoned by the young boys. The levees had failed, Katrina's devastation painfully accurate in this replica. I wished the boys were here so I could congratulate them on their accuracy. I also wanted to tell them how I, a mere citizen, had taken whatever steps I could to help. But the boys were gone, and all that remained was a much-diminished river as the water-soaked field slowly gave up its liquid burden to the asphalt and Sunday sunshine.

I had encountered a system that appeared indifferent and apathetic. In the case of Jim Brown, I had encountered a real live person who chastised me for my activism and treated me as a suspicious person and a nuisance. How, then, could I urge these boys to contact the authorities if this happened again? Besides, I don't know if they'd listen to me. Sprinkler guy would no doubt have more impact. After all, he's got the key!

Flight Crews Express Local Culture

We recently flew from Cincinnati to Seattle. It was a two-leg journey, as we had to change planes in Denver. We've noticed over the years that airports all look pretty much the same, with very little in the way of regional flavor. But, I've noticed that regional tone and style can be detected in the voices and speaking styles of the flight attendants from different cities. On this trip, for example, the flight attendants from Cincinnati sounded very different from the flight attendants in Denver. And their manner differed from the Seattle flight attendants, as well.

The Cincinnati airport is actually in Covington, Kentucky, so it's no surprise that the flight attendants often have a Southern, drawl. On this flight, for example, when I asked if I could have more ginger ale, the flight attendant said, "Why sure you can, sweetie!" She handed me my ginger ale with a big smile. This certainly was a contrast with the flight attendant we had when flying out from Seattle a week earlier. With Norwegian stoicism, she had handed me my drink with a grimace as if giving me poison for assisted suicide. True, I was sitting in a middle seat with no leg room and a broken tray table. And the seatbelt made me feel fat. But I still wanted to live!

Anyway, to return to the story of our return flights: We changed planes in Denver, trotting from gate 41 to gate 11, and availing ourselves of three different ambulators, people movers, or whatever those conveyor belts for human beings are called.

We got to our flight in time, even having a moment to grab up a copy of *The New York Times* that someone had discarded. Shuffling along in the line of boarding passengers, I read up on the latest outrageous words and acts of our despicable president, Trump. I couldn't wait to get on the plane and relax. At least we no longer had the anxiety of missing a plane. We would soon be at home sweet home.

So, the flight attendants from Denver did not have Southern accents, and moved just a bit more quickly, it seemed, though not necessarily more efficiently. The Colorado flavor and style would soon surface when a flight attendant came onto the intercom.

"Good evening," he said. "Welcome to Flight 242 to Chicago. Wait, um, flight 242 to Sea ..." He stopped mid-word and we could hear a shuffling of papers. Laughing just a bit, he continued, "Sorry about that. Flight 242 to Seattle."

As the passengers chuckled, just a bit nervously it seemed, we could hear the flight attendant stifling his own laughter, as a bevy of crewmates giggled nearby. I wondered how a flight attendant could be so confused about something as basic as where the plane was headed. John leaned over and whispered in my ear: "Marijuana is legal in Colorado."

Lead Paint, Vodka, and the Human Condition

I was standing in line at the customer service counter at my local grocery store, when the young man in front of me turned his head a couple of times and on the third time addressed me, in halting English, with this question, "Why does company put lead paint on toy?" He nodded toward a customer alert printed in huge type and taped to the customer service window.

"It makes the paint shiny," I said, sort of rolling my eyes to convey my disapproval of that particular technique.

"But what about common sense?" he asked. He gazed at me intelligently through wire-rimmed glasses. This man appeared young enough to be my grandson, and I would be proud to have a grandson who wasn't afraid to pose important questions, even to a stranger. Based on his accent, I surmised he might be from Russia. He shrugged his narrow shoulders and shook his head, repeating, "What about common sense?"

"Common sense can be used in different ways," I said. "I agree with you that it is common sense to protect children from poison. But pure capitalists believe it is common sense to make a bigger profit, no matter how you do it." He smiled and nodded, and I was instantly grateful that my time standing in line could be spent in one of my favorite pursuits: discussing political philosophy.

My new acquaintance was now leaning in closer to the alert so as to read the small print describing the toy train being recalled. Meanwhile, I became emboldened as my mind presented me with – alas, it is a passion! – political rhetoric. "That's why I'm a Democrat," I announced. Perhaps I could set him on what I considered *the enlightened path*! I spoke again: "Democrats believe that capitalism should be regulated in order to protect consumers." He appeared interested, so I continued: "Republicans often believe in pure unregulated capitalism. They think corporations should do whatever they can to increase their profits. It is up to the consumer to beware. But does it make sense for every mother to conduct a lead paint test on each toy she buys?"

I knew I was leaving out part of the standard justification for a free market economy. Republicans typically are convinced that eventually the market will self-correct. Consumers, they reason, eventually wise up and stop buying from companies that produce dangerous or defective products or from companies that pollute the environment.

But, of course, Republicans also tend to leave something out from the debate: they leave out the part about all the damage done before consumers recognize problems in products and services. Consumers don't always have a quick and effective way to vote with their pocketbooks. My main point stands: Democrats favor more regulation, Republicans less.

I've learned to make these little speeches with casual nonchalance since moving here to the sedate Northwest, more reserved than other places I've lived. In Texas and in the Midwest, for example, political debate could even crop up among women standing in line to use a public bathroom. And certainly on park benches, and at post offices and bus stops. And while living in Germany, I noticed how strangers freely give unsolicited opinions – even prescribing how a certain unruly child should be handled or when a specific yard should be mowed.

Perhaps this young man's national origins made him more open to conversations with strangers. He seemed, at the very least, as entertained by our dialogue as was I.

The customer service clerk, now just two customers away, glanced in our direction, but I doubted if she could hear us through the Plexiglas. Oh, well. I already knew her politics. Once when I was outside this store, arguing with a petitioner who was collecting signatures to do away with the "death tax," she had come came sprinting up to the petition table. On her way back inside from a cigarette break, she shouted toward the petitioner, "There's already a million dollar exemption for crying out loud. Rich people don't need more breaks!" Exactly the point I had been making that fine day.

So, the customer service clerk was a political ally, and I took comfort in suspecting she would side with me on this lead paint issue. At the very least, she must have been annoyed in recent days to have had her line clogged up with worried mothers returning shiny little trains.

Now it was the man's turn to return his purchase at the counter. As he did this, I busied myself with getting my receipts ready. My turn came next, and the clerk was quick and efficient. Soon I was on my way, sans package of unwanted merchandise. To my surprise, the man had paused.

"You say lead paint make toys shiny?" he asked.

"Yes," I replied. "Americans just love things that are bright and shiny. And now, we are literally being poisoned by the stuff that makes things bright and shiny!"

He chuckled. "That like in Russia, too, we have joke," he said. "We all drink vodka, we love vodka. We have joke that we crazy because we say same thing that make other people sick and die – make Russians healthy, live forever!"

We both broke into laughter. And for a moment, there we were, an American in her 60s, a Russian immigrant (I think) in his 20s, standing in the aisle at the grocery store, laughing our heads off at lead paint, vodka, and the perilous human condition.

At the Bar

John and I decided to stop in at a Thai restaurant where we'd eaten in the past. We weren't planning to eat there, but just have a drink. We had noticed this bar when we had eaten there in the past, and it seemed attractive and inviting, what with the amber lighting, the carved wood, and a couple of exotic plants.

We sidled up to the bar and slid onto a couple of bar stools. The bartender asked what we would like. John said he wanted a scotch on the rocks. I said I would like an *old fashioned*. The bartender looked confused, "A what?" he asked.

"An *old fashioned*," I repeated. "Can you make that?"

He frowned and said, "I've never heard of that. What's in it?"

I said, "Well, I think it has bourbon, bitters, and club soda. And some other things, maybe. And a cherry."

He looked amused, "I don't know," he said. "I typically just drink rum and coke. I don't know much about mixed drinks."

"But you're a bartender!" I pointed out.

"I'm new," he responded. Well, I guess.

The Lore of Stockings vs. the Chore of Pantyhose

The advent of pantyhose all but did away with stockings. At the same time, it introduced a topic for humor which, for some reason, stockings never did. I wonder why stockings are so serious and pantyhose so hilarious.

When first in vogue, many years ago, silk stocking were a luxury. They came in a special box, lined with tissue paper, an amorous gift from a significant other. Silk stockings, as seen now only in movies, were pulled onto shapely legs with dainty, well-manicured fingers. The seams were then flirtatiously straightened by the lady as her lover looked on with approval, if not outright lust. And, in magazine ads, the leg was always pointing demurely, as if at the North Star when it rises on a romantic night. So the lore around stockings is characterized by elegance, romance, and more than a hint of sexual innuendo.

Contrast the lore of stockings with the chore of pantyhose. These leg and derrière coverings come not in elegant boxes, but in cheap plastic bags, often three pairs for $2.79 or some such bargain price. No man in his right mind would present his beloved with a baggie of pantyhose – especially a man who has witnessed that most peculiar and definitely unsexy ritual of putting them on.

The problems of putting on pantyhose are myriad. First comes the issue of getting each respective leg into each respective leg portion. If one trics to put pantyhose on in the manner of socks – beginning with just one side – one is left with the other leg

59

portion of mesh dragging in an unseemly manner on the floor. Here the pantyhose leg portion joins the panty portion to which, as we know, it is attached – thus the name pantyhose. Which perhaps should be called hose panties since it is the hose part that must be mastered before the panty part even becomes an issue.

So, leaving that awkward logistic to the imagination, let's skip to the proper alignment of the panty. If either of the two leg portions were pulled on with less than perfect alignment, then the panties will be, as the expression goes, all in a twist. And if the ideal torque isn't applied, there will not be enough slack for the panty dance, consisting of jumping up and down while simultaneously doing the twist.

If the panty dance doesn't result in proper alignment, and it often doesn't, one must roll the hose back down and start all over again, this time pulling a little harder and stretching the fabric tighter. At which point the lady's beau, who has wisely chosen to stay in the other room, can be heard to say, "Hurry up or we'll be late. What are you doing in there, anyway?!"

The Endangered Greeting Card

I'd like to wax poetic about the humble greeting card. I think of it as an art form which, while marketed by gigantic corporations, still is created by gentle underpaid artists in their studios. As a child I got cards from my grandmother and from friends at my birthday parties. I couldn't bear to throw these cards away, so I saved them in a cigar box. In this digital age, when greetings are often online, I still treasure the endangered card even as I realize its days are numbered.

I enjoy browsing through the ever-changing card collections at the grocery store – working my way around the person who manages the collection like a museum curator – replacing old pieces with new ones. Even while dashing past the card aisle on my way to pick up a dozen eggs, I can spot a good card in my peripheral vision!

My addiction to cards started when I was about eight. I would pick up those free Hallmark date books that came out every January *wherever fine cards are sold.* I would carefully copy the birthdays of my friends and relatives from last year's book into the new one. When a birthday approached, I didn't have much access to "store-boughten" cards, so I would make them by hand. Even the envelopes.

By the time I was of double-digit age, I had progressed to commercial cards. Picking out a birthday card at the drugstore in our small town was a treat. In the same way that I was fascinated with comic strips, it was a ceaseless wonder to see how much could be conveyed through a picture not much bigger than a graham cracker. As a child, I paid scant attention to the words, just focusing on the visual theme. It was mostly a matter of *cute* – think ducklings or kittens in strange places like boots or wishing wells. Nature themes were also appealing – especially shooting stars and fields of poppies. That sort of thing.

You would think that as a writer I would disdain the commercial greeting card and write a heartfelt letter on plain linen paper. But when it comes to birthdays and holidays, I channel my grandmother, and buy cards. Granted, the cards I choose are often edgier than anything my grandmother would have chosen. For example, take the card I bought for one of my sons when he was a teenager: Outside: "When you were little, we used to take you to the park every week." Inside: "But somehow you always found your way home." Grandma would never have chosen a card like that. But we knew (and confirmed) that our son would appreciate the humor.

The cards that Grandma sent tended to be sentimental and affirming. In an attempt to live up to her image of me, I've made a lifelong effort to remember, and acknowledge, birthdays – not to mention Christmas, Father's Day, Mother's Day, and bereavement occasions. And thank you notes.

Now I also send cards on Easter, Thanksgiving, Halloween, Valentine's Day, and assorted anniversaries. It seems to me that the art, humor, and quality continue to evolve in charming ways.

Cute still wins points, especially for the cat people in my life. I already have a Thanksgiving card that I'm saving for my sister for next November. It shows a cat with its front paws propped on the table's edge, eyeing an unguarded turkey on a platter. How could I not get that. It is so her!

Valentine's Day cards are amazing – especially the Victorian ones with shiny embossed hearts and little boys in sailor hats riding huge tricycles. All those layers of lace and ribbon are just spectacular. I might add that my husband John usually springs for something to make me laugh, not swoon. This year, for example, the front of the card read, "You are *CALIENTE*! And inside it read, "With you, every day is Taco Tuesday!" Hey, that works for me!

My valentines to John range from the sentimental to the humorous. In the former category, I recently gave him a card that said, "The minute I heard my first love story, I started looking for you," a quote from Rumi. At the other end of the spectrum, I once sent him a card that read on the outside: "I more than love you ..." On the inside, it read, "I worship the floor you throw clothes on."

Yes, I sometimes choose a sarcastic card. I recently found a congratulations card for my nephew that he just loved. Outside: "When you go out into the world, you'll see how much of what you learned will be helpful and important." Inside: "Practically nothing."

Then there's the sarcastic Father's Day card I never mailed. Outside: "Dad, for Father's Day, I'd like to say those three words I don't say often enough." Inside: "Don't embarrass me."

I sometimes have trouble actually sending a sarcastic card. One card in my collection says, "So I forgot your birthday!" Inside: "So pick up the shattered pieces of your life and move on." Sounds great, I know, but I can't quite bring myself to mail it. Besides, I seldom forget a birthday.

Another unsent card in my collection begins, "Warning: This card contains language which may not be suitable for some family members." Inside, it reads, "Happing f_____ birthday!" Years ago, my sixth-grade son was looking through my collection of birthday cards. When he found that one, he thought it would be perfect for his friend who shared his sense of humor. One problem: The birthday boy's mother was a professor on my dissertation committee. I talked him into choosing another, tamer, card.

Easter cards crop up like spring vegetation. The fuzzy chicks, rabbits, and flowers that appear are enough to make you weep. And come fall, the Thanksgiving cards with their windswept autumn scenes, and glowing candles, fill me with warm nostalgia.

You have to be careful in choosing cards for people who are ill or recovering from surgery. If someone is suffering from a terminal disease, you don't want to send a card depicting a frog with a thermometer in its mouth or a mouse drinking chicken noodle soup. Likewise, if someone is just taking a few days of sick leave, you don't want to send a card that says, "We're with you at this difficult time and hope that happier healthier days are around the corner." It's just the flu, for God's sake!

You certainly don't want to make the mistake my cousin almost made. A friend of hers had just had a mastectomy, and Darlene got her a card that said, "So sorry for your loss." Fortunately, a friend intervened in time.

Sympathy cards can be so heartbreakingly beautiful that I won't even go there in this essay except to mention one designed for a bereaved pet owner: Outside: A black and white photograph of a lone dog sitting in the snow at the top of a hill, next to a fence. Inside: "No greater companion, no better friend."

Of course card companies invent card-giving occasions just to manipulate us into buying more cards. We now have Secretary's Day, Administrative Assistant's Day, Boss's Day, and a host of other special days. There are countless occasions I haven't even mentioned here – weddings, anniversaries, new babies, First Communion, Bar Mitzvah, Bat Mitzvah, Hanukkah, Passover, Kwanzaa, friendship, new house, *Bon Voyage.* The list goes on and on. Thus the category in my file: Miscellaneous.

Perhaps a card is the human's way of doing what a dog does – delivering a big slobbery kiss, resting a sympathetic head on the knee of a beloved one, or simply wagging one's tail to say, "So glad you are in my life."

When I send a card, I hope at the very least, to make someone I care about smile. I think that's what Grandma was doing, too.

Purging Catalogs from Our Mailbox to Combat Global Climate Change

Yikes! Something had to be done! The torrent of catalogs arriving in our mailbox each week had become almost unbearable. To fight back, I took to tearing off the back covers and systematically phoning each company to request being taken off their mailing list. This task was surprisingly pleasant and gave me a sense of accomplishment. All the customer relations people were friendly, and many said they understood completely. I even had an opportunity to mention global climate change to a few of them. Getting rid of catalogs was akin to pulling crabgrass – spotting those little nuisances and uprooting them one by one.

Of course, almost every customer relations person closed the conversation by saying it could take several months for the catalogs to cease, as many were "already in the pipeline."

While phoning 32 companies, I alphabetized the list so that when new catalogs arrived, I could quickly assess whether another phone call was indicated. After years of being horrified by the phrase, "Shop till you drop," I wondered if I had somehow become addicted to shopping without realizing it. I did sometimes head to the mall to spring loose from occasional funks and writer's blocks. Shopping for things one really needs is, of course, a necessity. But had shopping become not just a means to an end, but an end in itself? Had catalogs become a gateway drug to a shopping addiction?

I took a cold hard look at my list to honestly assess what I had been buying that might have led to this glut of shiny seductive catalogs. I was surprised to discover that I had, indeed, made purchases from about half of them. I had bought a singing teakettle from Crate and Barrel, dog vitamins from Drs. Foster and Smith, boots from Eddie Bauer, and yes, gifts from Harry and David. And there was that cheesecake that I bought for myself! Hardly something I needed!

Moving alphabetically down the list, I recalled buying rose bushes from Jackson and Perkins, a lampshade from Lamp's Plus, furniture covers from Lillian Vernon, a jacket from L.L. Bean, a car-visor-sun-zapper from Plow and Hearth, bean bag ottomans from Pottery Barn, and storage baskets (for my unfinished essays) from West Elm. And a few other purchases, most of which were not necessities. Meanwhile the catalogs seemed to metastasize.

I was glad I had called off so many companies before we left for our two-week vacation. But, when we returned, the accumulated mail still filled a huge plastic bin, and half the bulk consisted of catalogs – an average of two a day! I ripped off all the back covers, tossing the new harvest into our recycle bin with alacrity – fighting the impulse to check out that new "harp" end table from one company or the bird-motif fleece jacket from another. "Mustn't be tempted," was the refrain in my mind as I whisked each enticing offer out of sight.

Fifteen of this new crop were repeat offenders, and I put checkmarks on my list to so indicate. Yes, they had warned me this would happen, but I was going to keep close tabs just in case another phone call was necessary. (I noticed that I had *two* new catalogs from Pottery Barn, a company with, apparently, an unusually long and prolific pipeline.)

I was beginning to wonder if this catalog purge was ever going to pan out. The problem seemed intractable. I had hoped to illustrate how easy it is to simplify one's life while saving trees and cutting down on fossil-fuel energy used to publish and transport catalogs to our homes – and to subsequently schlep all this paper to recycling centers. When, if ever, could I report success?

And then it happened. Last Thursday, I went to my mailbox, and I found it! A tidy stack of mail, small enough to easily fit in one hand while I held the dog's leash in the other. Usually, embarking on a walk with my dog, I would rifle through the contents of the mailbox with one hand and then leave it there – the mail, not the hand – until I had walked Toby and taken him back inside. Then, I would return to the mailbox and use both hands to haul the unwieldy mass of flyers, catalogs, and mail into the house – sometimes having to chase down a wayward flyer blowing down the street. But halleluiah! Today's mail was a beautiful little stack of envelopes. Not a single catalog.

Oh, I know that the battle is not yet won. I know there will be hard days ahead – days when the mailbox again sports an untidy stack of catalogs. Days when I have to phone 15 more companies. There may even be a day when I have to gird up my loins and phone Pottery Barn and ask them just how long their pipeline is, for heaven's sake! This is a marathon, not a sprint.

But on Thursday the inside of my mailbox looked like one of those pictures one sees on a holiday card. The feeling that swept over me was downright nostalgic. It was a Currier and Ives moment. My mail was simply mail. How pretty. How quaint. How simple. And I like to think that somewhere in the Northwest, a branch of a tree has been saved and is absorbing CO_2 that would otherwise go into the atmosphere – an atmosphere that most decidedly does not need it. And I hope that a little less gasoline will be pumped into delivery and garbage trucks for my dubious benefit. And that, as a result of all this, a cubic inch of ice in Antarctica will remain frozen, as it should be, and not melt away into the rising and troubled sea.

Procrastination

My husband accuses me of being a procrastinator, but I don't think I am. It's true that I often defer tasks to a later date, but this is simply a matter of prioritizing. I have a bit of a triage concept when it comes to focusing on this or that.

Having said that, I will admit that I do have a tendency to do the small, easy, mindless tasks before sitting down to engage in the more complex ones. It's far easier to sort laundry, for example, than to figure out if and when I should see a doctor about a particular issue.

Writers are notorious for washing every last dish, removing every last cobweb, and trimming their cat's claws before sitting down to confront an empty page or a humming computer.

I'd like to say more about this, but I can't right now because I just noticed that my African violet could probably use a bit more water.

When He Was Younger

Recently my husband, John, and I returned from a quick visit to California to check in with our son, Nick, his wife, Chi Hyon, and their son, Adrian. These visits are really all about our four-year-old grandson! We cherish every minute with this little boy, and are grateful that we've been able to visit him almost every month since he was born. This visit was special because he and his mother, who is from Korea, were about to leave for a two-month visit to her native country.

The last time Adrian visited his relatives in Korea was a year ago, when he was three. Now, when we talk to him about being there, he says he can't remember very much. Of course, he always has a great time during his annual visits to Korea. But, like any four-year-old, he doesn't have great recall about things he did a whole year earlier. John and I decided to help him build up excitement about the upcoming trip. "You'll get to see your Korean cousins and practice your Korean!" I said.

"I don't really know Korean," he said. "I used to know it – but that was when I was younger." That just cracked us up. Here was a four-year-old lamenting the lost skills of his youth.

And how quickly the years fly by. It seems that he was born so recently. Yet he is about to graduate from preschool. On the last day of this most recent visit, I spent the morning at Adrian's school. Toward the end of the morning, they gathered for circle time. They were invited to take turns pantomiming an animal. A little girl imitated a cat, a little boy a tiger, and so forth.

I was pleasantly surprised to see Adrian pipe up, "I have one!" Last time I had visited his preschool, he had hung back from activities like this. But now he was a willing, even enthusiastic, participant.

Entering the circle, he shaped each hand into a three-fingered claw. With elbows bent and claws raised, he stomped across the small space.

One little girl guessed, "A dinosaur?"

"Yes!" he said, clearly pleased. "But which one?"

He continued his journey back and forth, surrounded by the circle of classmates.

"A brontosaurus?" ventured a little boy.

"No, I have spikes on my tail!"

"A T Rex?" This from a boy who jumped up as he ventured his guess.

"No, I'm not that big!" said Adrian.

"A pterodactyl?"

"No, I can't fly!" And so it proceeded with Adrian continuing to stomp back and forth, "claws" extended. Here's a kid who really knows his dinosaurs! But unless there was another dinosaur expert in the class, this could go on for a very long time!

"What letter does it start with?" I offered.

"An A," he said.

Whew! I was glad he knew that. After all, they're just learning the initial letters of certain words.

A little girl promptly shouted, "An allosaurus!"

"Right!" he said, breaking into a big smile. It was a moment I hope to remember for a long time.

When the children lined up to go out for recess, it was time for me to take off. In the past, Adrian used to cling to me, plead with me to stay, even cry. But this time, his protests quickly died down when I assured him his grandpa and I would pick him up in a few hours.

As the class filed out of the room, I gathered up the books I had brought and read aloud. I was proud of my grandson, but also a bit sad that he was growing up so fast.

I made my way down the hall and into the foyer, the area where John and I typically pick Adrian up after school when we're in town. In this foyer is a huge aquarium where our ritual is for the three of us to pause and say our goodbyes to the fish. Adrian likes to spot his favorites – Goldie, Angel, and Cat. To find them, we must all squat down and peer into a variety of fishy hiding places within and behind the aquarium sculptures.

When the fish wave their tails, Adrian interprets this as a "Goodbye." We cheerfully go along with his assessment. Then we proceed to the door where Adrian smiles and waves at the doorman/security guard. As we walk outside, Adrian says to him, "Thank you," and then, "Bye bye." Our grandson is clearly proud of his growing social skills.

As I walked outside, I realized that when John and I picked Adrian up later that day, it would probably be our last time for this beloved ritual, at least at this school. Soon Adrian would be on his way to Korea, and when he returned to California, he would be preparing to start Kindergarten at another location.

I felt sad that the preschool era was coming to a close. As grandparents, John and I have used these monthly visits to build a strong relationship with our grandson. Typically, we have taken Adrian to our San Jose rental house where he has his own room – although the entire house is a playscape! We have worked together to build train tracks and run toy trains. Or, to build towers with blocks. We've also played with play dough and puzzles, and drawn together with crayons and markers. We've read books together and even cooked a few things!

In inclement weather, a favorite destination has been the San Jose Children's Museum, an amazing place! But when the weather is nice, we often play in our back yard – perhaps in the sandbox or in a play pool. We'll sometimes pretend to be dinosaurs, chasing each other with wild roars! We run with him – or after him – as he rides his bike around the block. We've seen him progress from his Thomas the Train minicycle to a Batman tricycle to a two-wheeler with training wheels.

We also embark on outings to playgrounds and parks, and to the occasional ice cream store. The highlight for Adrian used to be to go down slides. Now it's to ride his two-wheeler. During this latest visit, he thrilled to ride this bike through deep puddles from a recent rainfall.

One day, when the temperatures in San Jose soared into the 90s, we made an impromptu trip to an ocean beach an hour's drive away. In Capitola, the temperatures were at least 15 degrees cooler – so cool in fact that I myself chose to nestle on towels laid out on the warm sand, a bit protected from the ocean breezes. There I watched Adrian and John run toward the receding waves and then race back toward shore, with riotous shouts, when the crashing waves rolled back in as if chasing them.

It was wonderful to watch grandson and grandfather frolicking together. When Adrian eventually became chilly, he ran to me, and I wrapped him in a warm towel, holding him tight and savoring the moment. I offered him the little bag of airline pretzels still in my purse. After downing these, he jumped up and ran off to help some nearby kids build a sand castle.

We don't know how much he'll remember about these experiences, but that's the way it goes.

Each time that we drop Adrian off at his house and then make our way down the long driveway, we call out from the car, 'We love you!" He shouts after us, "I love you more." And then we beep the horn two times.

John and I plan to keep these visits going for as long as our health holds out. But, Adrian's not the only one getting older. Time is flying for us, too, and it's getting harder for us to sprint after this energetic boy when he's on his bike. Or to run and hide behind trees when we play hide-and-seek. So far, we manage to keep up, but we're increasingly aware that these days will eventually come to a close.

Adrian's other grandfather has already passed away. His grandmother in Korea is doing well, but she, too, is slowing down.

Like the dinosaurs, we grandparents will not last forever.

Some day, hopefully a long time off, a friend might ask Adrian, "Do you have grandparents?"

And he might say, "I used to. We had a lot of fun together. But that was when I was younger."

Toddler Discovers Tools!

At about the age of one, a child may become especially attached to a favorite toy – perhaps a stuffed animal, a rattle, a little truck, or a doll. So, it was no surprise when my grandson Carter developed a favorite toy. What was a bit surprising was his choice: Carter fell in love with a shovel!

This particular shovel was yellow plastic. It was part of a little beach toy set I had purchased for him when I saw it on sale at the end of the summer of 2017. In addition to the shovel, there was a little wagon, about the size of a wide shoe box. I knew that there were no beach trips coming up any time soon. But, I thought Carter might enjoy pulling some of his little toys around in the wagon. The shovel, I figured, would be of lesser interest.

When I went to visit him shortly after giving him this little set, his other grandmother said, "He loves the shovel you gave him. He can even say shovel!" I noticed that Carter was indeed holding the plastic shovel. His grandmother pointed to it and asked, "What is this, Carter?"

"Sho-vel!" he said with enthusiasm.

This made me laugh. Carter only knew about five words at this point – *Mama, Dada, bottle, byebye*, and now *shovel*!

Carter had turned one that July, he walked confidently, and as he toddled here and there, he now almost always had this little shovel clutched in one hand. He sometimes dragged or pushed the shovel along the hardwood floors, as if delighted with his mastery of this tool. He liked the little wagon, too, but it just couldn't compete with his love for the shovel.

For several months, Carter didn't shovel anything, but just seemed intrigued with the way this tool extended his reach. As he walked around his play areas, he would use the shovel to poke at things and to explore the spaces to be found under or behind the sofa or other pieces of furniture. He also used his shovel to gently bang or tap on various surfaces as if studying the different sounds he could produce.

Carter's love of this shovel quickly led to an affection for other tools, or even just sticks. When outdoors, he frequently picked up a stick and carried it around until some adult gently talked him into putting it back down so he could go on a swing, get back in the car, hold his bottle, or whatever.

When my husband John and I got him a drum, he loved the drumsticks. Not content to simply bang on the drum, he used the drumsticks much as he had the shovel, simply enjoying how they extended his reach. He would reach up to bang on the top of the kitchen counter, bang on a door handle, bang on a sliding glass door, and so forth.

When Carter learned to run and gallop, we had to be more cautious. But under adult supervision, he still had plenty of time to play with his shovel and a variety of sticks. He began to show a preference for holding them in his right hand but was remarkably adept with either hand.

One day we brought him a backscratcher, and he was thrilled. He promptly took it all over the house, poking it into crevices

– the space under a closed door, the window of a toy truck, the open grid of a safety gate – as if putting this new tool through its paces: "Let's see what this baby can do!"

On another day, while he was at our house, I held him as he perched on the kitchen counter. He spotted the container of kitchen tools – spatulas, wooden spoons, whisks, tongs, and so forth. His eyes widened with astonishment as if he had just discovered the mother lode of tools. Not shovels, that's true. But perhaps somehow related in his mind. He lunged toward the tools. I held him safely, but handed him a smooth-edged spatula.

After examining the spatula for a moment, he held it aloft, like the Statue of Liberty, a mischievous grin playing on his face. He then proceeded to push the spatula around on the counter, similar to the way he liked to use his shovel on wood floors. I let him explore all the other kitchen tools that were safe enough for him to handle.

When he showed interest in the meat mallet, I got out some play dough and let him pound away. Hammers and play dough are now mainstays in his playtime options. And, boy can he bang away!

A few weeks before Christmas, Carter accompanied us to the Christmas tree farm where we go to cut down our own tree. All bundled up, we made our way down a dirt road to the patch of trees that were available for harvest. John carried the saw that he would use to saw down our selection. Carter, of course, wanted to hold the saw, or at least touch it. But, because of its sharp teeth, John kept it safely away from the reach of this determined little boy.

We selected a tree, and John knelt to saw it down. Time for a photo op! John continued to keep the sharp part of the saw well away from Carter. But, Carter managed to get his hand on the curved handle. The photograph shows Carter's obvious delight; he was touching the saw! He looked like the proverbial cat with the canary. Who needs Christmas trees?! But, saws – that's another matter!

On Christmas day, Carter and his cousin Adrian were at our house when snow blanketed the neighborhood. "Let's go build a snowman!" we all said. We dressed one-and-a-half year old Carter and four-and-a-half year old Adrian in their winter jackets, hats, and mittens. Outside, Carter's father, Adrian's father, and I all began rolling snowballs and trying to engage the little ones in the process of building a snowman.

But, Carter's attention was riveted elsewhere: he was watching his grandfather clearing snow from the driveway with – you guessed it – a shovel! Carter insisted on having a chance to hold the shovel and push it through the snow. His cousin seemed equally interested in the shoveling operation. For both boys, the snowman project took a backseat to this opportunity to use a shovel!

Of course, we've provided Carter with various things that he can scoop up or shovel – buttons, plastic eggs, magnetic letters. And at the playground, he plays with sand, dirt, leaves, and bark chips – all at the mercy of whatever shovel or stick he has at the time.

Carter's love of tools made it a slam dunk for him to learn to use a spoon. In fact, he tolerated being fed for only a very short time before insisting that he himself hold the spoon or fork. Just yesterday, he was using a little spoon to feed himself oatmeal with milk and blueberries. He was having a bit of trouble getting a plump blueberry onto his spoon. "Pretend your spoon is a shovel!" I offered. That bit of encouragement apparently did the trick, as he soon was successful in getting the blueberry to his mouth.

One evening, I put about a dozen plastic eggs in a big mixing bowl and gave Carter a huge serving spoon with which to stir the eggs. This soon led to his wanting to scoop or shovel up the eggs. So, I gave him another bowl to transfer the eggs to. For about an hour, he scooped the eggs from one bowl to the other and back again, intent on using the spoon.

A couple of weeks ago, Carter and Adrian, along with other family members, rode up Crystal Mountain in a shiny red gondola. Carter was visibly excited as our gondola drifted silently upward into the winter clouds. We gently rocked to and fro as the wind picked up and the snow fell faster. Looking out the windows, we gazed at the beautifully frosted trees surrounding us! It was thrilling to be transported to another world. Carter, sitting on his father's lap, turned this way and that, saying, "Trees! Trees!"

At the top of the mountain, we debarked, walked up a slope to a restaurant, and had a snack before returning to get on what Carter called the 'gah'lala.'

When we got to the bottom, we all quickly climbed off as the attendant held the door open. "The exit's over here!" called John. But Carter was insisting on a different route: He had spotted a rack of snow shovels!

This sweet little boy had just had the rare opportunity to drift over a forest of pine trees during a blizzard. Exciting, no doubt.

But gondola excursions pale when compared to a collection of shovels!

I don't know where this love of tools will lead. Will Carter be a drummer? A surgeon? A hockey player? An archaeologist? When you think about it, tools are a way of extending and expanding the capacity of the human arm and hand. So, perhaps he will go into robotics. It's impossible to predict what his future will be. Meanwhile, I look forward to having a grandson who – just maybe – will enjoy raking our leaves, shoveling our snow, and maybe even stirring the stew! But only after he has practiced playing his violin!

My Vintage Computer

One day, my computer froze solid, displaying an alarming pattern of a zillion rectangles. Yikes! It wasn't unattractive – resembling as it did something one might see at a museum of modern art. It wasn't the dreaded blue screen of death, but perhaps its modern counterpart. The pattern eclipsed all the icons, making the computer inoperable except for the off switch.

I phoned the support line where the representative said it sounded like the graphics card might be failing – and set me up with an appointment at an authorized service center.

Gritting my teeth, I accepted this grim diagnosis and treatment plan. The appointment was for late afternoon the following Tuesday. Hoping to avoid evening rush hour, I asked, "Are there any morning appointments?"

"You can contact the service center directly and change the time," she said.

So, I phoned the service center. "We have plenty of morning appointments," chirped the clerk. "But …" Her tone suddenly darkened, like a cloud eclipsing the sun. After an ominous pause, she said, "I see a problem."

"Uh oh!" I said, gazing dolefully at my frozen screen. *Now what?*

"Based on your computer's serial number, I see it's vintage. We no longer service vintage computers."

Vintage? Vintage?! The word *vintage* struck me as a kind of hippie word, applied to long, patterned dresses with oversized buttons. We hip computer users walk right past vintage stores, our visionary eyes focused on the sleek futuristic silver and white computer stores – the furthest thing from vintage.

"How old is it?" I asked, nervously twisting the string of 50s beads I was wearing. Okay, I do sometimes go vintage.

"Well, you bought it in 2012, but it was built in 2011." She made it sound like it was a true relic – something found in the attic, no doubt covered in cobwebs and old bird nests. Sitting next to a butter churn.

"But, it's only seven years old!" I protested. Did they really think that using the fancy word *vintage* would soften the blow of telling me I'm hopelessly behind?

"How old does a computer have to be to be considered vintage?" I asked.

"Five years," she said – with great confidence – as if her answer actually made sense.

Five years?! Five. So, that's the way it's going to be, eh?

I said my goodbyes, hung up the phone, and switched off my computer. I would forget about doing any writing today. I had a better plan. I would play with my little grandson. He recently turned five. You know, *vintage*.

Note: I was invited to read this piece for KQED Radio, in San Francisco, as part of their Perspectives series. It aired on September 28, 2018.

How Not to Accept a Compliment

When I get a compliment, I rarely respond the way I should. I know, for example, that if someone says, "I like your sweater," you are supposed to smile and say, "Why, thank you!" And leave it at that.

But, if someone compliments me on my sweater, I'm apt to launch into a dissertation about the sweater. "This old thing?!" I begin. "It is such a weird shade that I hardly ever wear it. But my sister-in-law gave it to me, so I feel compelled to keep it. If you look closely, you'll see moth holes. The moths certainly like it!"

At this point, I begin frantically searching for the moth holes – to prove my point. Not readily locating these, I proceed to remove the sweater to pursue my search.

By this time, the well-intentioned person may have fled. But if the person is still there, I next thrust the sweater out and say, "Here. Would you like it? I know it's a weird color, but it matches your eyes."

And that's how not to accept a compliment.

My Life With Insects

Sprawled out on the crabgrass in our Ohio back yard, I watched a tiny inch worm curl its pale green body, then furl out on a stem to repeat its acrobatics till it reached a confusion of leaves Such magic! While my sisters were content to play indoors, I took every opportunity to skip out the door and get down in the dirt.

How insects captured my attention! Even photographs of me as a child show me crouched on the ground, my cornsilk hair mingling with the antennae of my latest find.

Ohio insects were the best. I could not believe my eyes the first time I saw a praying mantis, its spindly body looking like it was assembled of mini TinkerToys. Then there were the walking sticks, mimicking the twigs on which they perched. Spotting such a creature, I would run for an empty peanut butter jar, stuff it with leaves, and capture my find for further observation.

I loved to pry up a rock and see what lived beneath, watching "rollie pollies" become tiny pellets in my palm. Centipedes also hid out under rocks, and although I marveled at their multitude of legs, I gave them a wide berth.

Feeling a piercing pain, I would look up to see a smug bumblebee circling the site of the crime. I tended to forgive bees, because they were hard workers and had something to do with making flowers bloom and making honey to eat.

The ladybug, red with black polka dots, looked as if designed by a child with a box of Crayolas.

Many Ohio spiders build exquisite webs, just like the star of E.B. White's *Charlotte's Web*. Familiar with that story, I was fond of spiders. Finding one in the bathtub, I would gently nudge it into a jar, using a matchbook cover. Then I would take it outdoors and release it.

Meanwhile I admired the butterflies drifting through the air like tiny paintings entertaining invisible angels. Monarch butterflies were common, and at school we kept cocoons of them on the science shelf where we could watch them emerge each spring.

Midwestern evenings brought out the night shift of insects. In the fading pink of a Midwestern sunset, lightning bugs began to glimmer like stars sifting down from the heavens. My parents would sit on the porch gazing into the shadows, as my sisters and I ran about, catching these phosphorescent miracles. And a chorus of crickets on a summer night still evokes that feel of being a child, safe in the embrace of my house, my yard, my family, and my town.

My parents and teachers taught me respect, and even awe, for the wonders of nature. But when I became an adult, I unfortunately assumed a pragmatic stance toward insects. As a responsible parent and homeowner, I turned into an insect vigilante intent on keeping them at bay.

In Washington, D.C., I swatted at flies and sprinkled hot chili powder on the aphids intent on consuming our tomatoes before we could! In Denver, I fanned bees and wasps out of windows, and put down ant poison. In California, I applied the death penalty to black widow spiders that hid out under the seats of my children's tricycles. I took a broom to wasp nests and then ran like crazy to the shelter of my house.

In New Hampshire, I lured mosquitoes to lamps that incinerated them with a noisy buzz. And I rejoiced after smashing a bloody mosquito on my flesh. I starved gypsy moth caterpillars by ringing trees with foil so they could not reach their leafy dinner.

In Texas, I protected my children from the fire ant hills that cropped up in our yard. This, too, involved the application of poison. I poured toxic mothballs into boxes of stored clothing and mercilessly smashed moths, quickly removing the telltale powder from the wall. I committed all these brutalities, and at times with loathing and glee.

So firmly had I been in this adult mode of thinking that I was caught off guard one day when I noticed a small boy kneeling on the sidewalk and gazing intently at something on our lawn. I wondered what he saw. A bit later, I saw that he had returned with a glass jar. He gently picked up a stick on which a praying mantis was perched, and put it in an empty peanut butter jar. Then he carefully put the jar in the little case on the back of his bike.

I guessed that he would take this magnificent creature home and show it to his mother. He would stare at it with curiosity and wonder. He would give it a few drops of water. And then, not knowing what to give it for dinner, he would let it go.

As the boy rode off, I returned to the kitchen. I thought wistfully of my Ohio childhood and its insects. I gazed at the fruit flies newly dancing above my peaches and pears. Pulling up a stool, I sat down and stared. And I was filled, once again, with awe.

Klaxon Alarm

We were in Spain, John and I, sleeping soundly in a small old hotel on the outskirts of Madrid when we were rudely awakened by an ear-shattering alarm in our room. It was a klaxon. We leaped from our bed with the shared conclusion: "Fire! We've got to evacuate!" I searched for my jacket and shoes, as John advised, "Hurry! These old hotels go up like tinderboxes!"

I got out into the hallway before him, because it took him a second longer than I to find his shoes. The hall was quiet as a snowy night, even though the alarm in our room still screeched loudly. And, there was no action in the hall – no people emerging from rooms in their pajamas and bolting for exits. All was calm.

"There's no alarm out here," I shouted to John, my voice competing with the ongoing klaxon alarm that continued to make our room uninhabitable.

An investigation was in order. John quickly located the source of the sound – our new so-called "smart phone"! It was set to wake us up at 7:00 AM the next morning, but it had somehow come unplugged and was apparently programmed to warn us that the battery might not last till then. John managed to silence it, and we sank onto our bed, relieved but not quite ready to laugh!

Had we woken up others in our tour group? We debated what to tell our traveling companions at breakfast if anyone mentioned the loud noise from somewhere on the third floor. We considered feigning ignorance or donning a puzzled expression and muttering, "Yeah, we heard it too! Wonder what that was!"

But, as we climbed back into bed, our smart phone securely plugged in this time, we decided we would come clean. At breakfast, not a word was said, so we remained mum.

I blush to admit that it happened again in Granada. Again, no mention made!

Barefoot and Baffled
at the Dawn of Computers

When it comes to computers, I'm not what is called an early adopter. These days I use my computer to produce books and videos, edit photographs, write essays, send emails, and access websites. I have a blog and am webmaster of two websites. But the journey has not been easy.

I headed to college with the same old typewriter my father had used in graduate school. This was one of those old black Remingtons with a semicircle of letters mounted at the ends of slender metal levers. This stood me, as the saying goes, in good stead for close to a decade. I used it throughout college, and then carried it with me, in its worn black case, as I moved from college to various jobs and on to graduate school.

It was, in fact, sitting on a table in my apartment when a very special date came for dinner. Soon, I was married to John, and changed my last name to Tornow. My trusty old typewriter was among the cases and bundles we moved into our first home.

During those early years of marriage, and starting a family, I worked as an office temp and discovered the wonder of Selectric typewriters. I longed to have one of my own, so when I managed to sell our first house, without having to use a realtor, we took several hundred dollars from our savings and plopped it down for what was, at the time, an incredible luxury. My own Selectric! In ocean blue!

Meanwhile computers were being invented in the garages of geniuses like Bill Gates and Steve Jobs. I heard a bit about this, but knew in my heart that nothing could surpass Selectrics.

When John got stationed in Germany for the Air Force, I left my heavy Selectric with my mother, urging her to write a family history, or at least the story of her own life. Alas, she never found the time, and the typewriter just sat in the guest room for years until it finally made its way to Goodwill.

In Germany, I felt lost without my Selectric, but it wouldn't even have worked on European 220-volt power. One day I saw an ad in the *Stars and Stripes* newspaper for a European Selectric being sold by a German Air Force officer. John and I drove to his home and struck a deal. Although I was delighted with the purchase, I was taken aback by the handshake of the officer as we were leaving. He crunched my fingers in such a tight handshake that I was afraid I might never type again. But my hand was all right, and I spent many hours in the following months writing away on my Selectric after the kids were asleep.

By this time, computers were taking the U.S. by storm, although not so much among military families living abroad. During our mid-tour trip home to Ohio, John and I went to a computer store to see what all the fuss was about. The eager young salesman showed us some software that would enable children to see, through little movies, how the heart works, how storms develop, and so forth. We took the leap and ordered our first computer.

Two months later, when the computer arrived in Germany, John hauled the box up the two flights of stairs to our third floor bedroom. (The house was tall and narrow, and living in it was like living in a tree house.) With great gusto, John tore open the box and began flailing the Styrofoam blocks and the bubble wrap hither and yon as he pulled forth the jewel he had been so long awaiting.

The cat quickly crawled into the empty box and lay down as our young boys began jumping up and down on the bubble wrap to make it pop. John began poring over the manual with obvious fascination. This was back in the days when one had to insert floppy discs and install operating systems, and stuff like that.

I stood back a bit, taking in the whole scene. I cast a wistful eye at my trusty Selectric, now shoved unceremoniously to a shadowy corner. Did I mention that Selectrics have these adorable little metal orbs covered with all the letters of the alphabet? And that these orbs swivel, bob, and strike according to what letter you press? It's really quite ingenious. And you can switch out orbs when you want a different font.

But, back to our story. Peering up from the manual, John asked if I would go downstairs and fetch us some tea. Yes, tea, that would be good I thought, grateful to turn my attentions to a task I felt up to. As I started down the first flight of stairs, John called out, "You can make it in the new microwave." Our first microwave had arrived in that same shipment. As I started down the second flight of stairs, he called out, "You just heat the water for a minute on high, I think." And, as I reached the first floor, he added, "Be sure to plug it in first." He knows me well.

I filled two mugs with water and approached the virginal microwave taking up an inordinate amount of counter space in our tiny kitchen. I stared at the buttons and dials. Finally, I discovered that the door would swing open if I pushed a small button that said "Stop." I put the mugs inside and snapped the door shut. Now what? Clueless and overwhelmed by the multiplicity of instruction manuals I would eventually have to read, I pushed "stop" again and took the mugs out. I poured the water into a saucepan and placed it over a burner, turning the flame to high. Serenely, I watched the water as tiny bubbles began to form.

Just then, John came bounding down the stairs and into the kitchen. There I stood, barefoot and baffled on the worn wooden floor, staring dolefully at the flames darting up around my little pot of water. My patient husband smiled and cast his eyes toward the microwave and back at me. He shrugged as I poured the scalding water into the mugs. I braced myself for his comment: "You look like you've returned to the Stone Age!"

"Yes," I said, acknowledging his ironic jest. "But, there's something comforting about simply boiling water in a pan. Tonight I'll do this, and tomorrow, I'll woman up and get with the program." Sipping my tea, I knew I could do it, in time. I could lean into yet another steep learning curve. But tonight the old technologies were working just fine. Flame. Pan. Water. Mug. No instruction manual needed.

Trump's Signature

Have you seen Trump's signature? I first noticed it during the televised Congressional questioning of his former personal attorney, Michael Cohen. Cohen had brought certain documents to the hearings to substantiate his claims of Trump's complicity in illegal behavior. In this case, Cohen presented a photo of a check for $40,000, partial payment for hush money for porn star, Stormy Daniels.

The check was shown on TV in such close-up that it filled our wide screen TV. Trump's signature in the lower right corner was just weird. If you didn't know already that it said Donald Trump, you would never know.

It was a scribble of, I guess, letters that were all squished together as if his name had been caught between closing elevator doors: DonaldTrump. Or, you know how sometimes on documents, there's a short little line, half the length of a paperclip, where you're supposed to just put your initials? But somebody like Trump, who can't read, would try to put his whole name there – and it ends up being compressed like an accordion – you know, an accordion when all the air has been pushed out.

If Trump's signature depicted a mountain range, it would be mountains so treacherous no one would want to climb them or even look at them from afar. The mountain peaks in his signature look like places where demons and vultures would hang out, screeching menacingly into thin air.

Or maybe his signature resembles, even more closely, what you see on a heart monitor next to someone's bed in the cardiac unit. It looks like some weird type of tachycardia, signaling a failing heart. It makes sense when you think about it, because Trump appears to have no heart – just some sort of facsimile that can pump some blood, but not big enough to hold anything like compassion or love.

Trump does not round any of his letters, not even the *n* in *Donald* or the *m* in *Trump*. Instead, every single letter is rendered sharp and pointed, like a switchblade. I know he grew up in the Bronx, but do all the letters have to be so jagged and piercing? Does he have to weaponize everything – even the letters in his name?

Meanwhile, Americans who are paying attention are aghast at the cruelty of our president. Many wonder, *How could anyone be so malicious? How did America lose its moral compass and end up with a president who uses his power to do so much harm – to literally kill children, democratic institutions, and the environment?* Trump once even bragged about killing hope – when he was announcing policies to prevent asylum seekers from trying to enter the United States. And he does it all with lies. He kills truth itself.

On April 29, 2019, the *Washington Post's* Fact Checker determined that Trump had hit the "dubious milestone of 10,000 false or misleading claims since he started his presidency." They went on to say that his average is 12.2 false claims per day. You know what? I think Trump's signature replicates the pattern that appears on the screen of a lie detector. A lie detector exposes lies. And Trump's signature exposes who he is: a pathological liar.

Trump has plastered his name on buildings and golf courses around the world. But his signature reminds us of the man behind the myth. A man who is cruel, dishonest, sadistic, and violent. A man with no love or music in his heart. A man without a soul.

Massive HRT Withdrawal Portends Doom

For years now, drug companies have been telling doctors to tell women that hormone replacement therapy (HRT) was good for their hearts. But when the drug companies actually looked at the research, they were amazed to find that HRT was not *good* for women's hearts, but in fact *bad*. With thousands of women suddenly abandoning HRT, we can expect a breakdown in the country's infrastructure which will make the collapse of the stock market look like a mere game of pick-up sticks.

A spokesperson from Wymont Pharmaceuticals, who wished to remain anonymous, said, "You could have knocked me over with a feather. I mean, like Who knew?!" He added that he was quite grateful for the fortuitous "whim" that led him to sell his own Wymont stocks just hours before the research findings were released to the media.

Women across the country are tossing bottles of HRT down their garbage disposals with abandon. Marine biologists predict that the resulting surge of hormones in the nation's sewers will eventually appear in fish. Research into the effects of trace amounts of HRT on fish-eating *men* is well underway. A vaccine for *men* should be available by next Friday.

Meanwhile, night sweats and insomnia are preventing millions of women, and by turn their mates, from getting needed sleep. The highway department is noting a significant increase in local fender-benders and interstate pileups as sleep-deprived, semi-conscious citizens attempt to operate automobiles, SUVs, trucks, and buses.

Millions of women, who have been calm for close to a decade now, are again railing against the failure of men to read their minds, remember important dates, and replace spent toilet paper spools.

With thousands, if not millions, of suddenly edgy women showing up for work at offices, factories, and retail outlets from coast to coast, the atmosphere in these locations is expected to become highly charged, if not hostile, with the result that the gross national product is expected to fall precipitously.

Alan Greenspan will be issuing a statement later this week after he attends his wife's 40th high school reunion, something he had previously thought he could get out of.

Men, long the target of edgy women, are advised to stay indoors and to avoid communication via language of any kind, including body language. The failure to communicate may also be a problem.

A public service announcement currently being aired on all major networks advises all males to keep a low profile. Any male who spots beads of sweat on the forehead of a woman is urged to seek shelter immediately. Some local communities are converting public school auditoriums into temporary shelters for men (and other "insensitive" persons) until this crisis passes.

Because many women occupy positions in local and state government, a breakout of internecine warfare amongst states and municipalities is expected. National Guard units have been called to their duty stations, something which has really pissed off their wives who are sick and tired of waiting for the boxes of holiday decorations, which have been sitting in the hall since New Year's Day, to be hauled back up to the attic – for God's sake! Some wives were heard muttering that they guessed they would just have to do it themselves.

Zoologists report that the shrieks of women in coastal cities are already disrupting the ability of pods of whales to communicate via sonar. Schools of dolphins are also showing a loss in ability to navigate until things quiet down.

Meteorologists predict that the collective hot flashes and night sweats will soon increase atmospheric humidity and temperature so as to bring about another *El Niño* – and this one will be more severe than that of a few years ago. Geologists are keeping a close watch on the glaciers via satellite monitoring.

Further advisories at www.IamNOTbeingunreasonable!com

How I Paid $90 for a Cup of Coffee

Many of us can remember when coffee was 25 cents a cup – that is, on the rare occasions when we purchased coffee by the cup. Generally, we consumed coffee we made ourselves, at home, in our percolators and later from drip coffeemakers. But occasionally, we shelled out 25 cents at a fast food counter, a bus station, a sports event, or a tourist destination. A quarter for a cup seemed reasonable, as we fed our craving for that black brew that smelled so good and gave us that little punch of energy.

And because coffee is so good, and our bodies and taste buds appreciate it so much, we have been good sports about the price increases – from 25 cents to 35 cents to 50 cents to 75 cents, and eventually breaking the one-dollar barrier. Once businesses saw that we would pay even a dollar a cup, they were quick to boost the price to $1.50, even $2.00. Occasionally, some of us even coughed up $3.50 for a cup of java – while at the opera or some out of the way place where water had to be hauled in or reclaimed through nearby desalinization plants.

The turn of the century brought about a revolution in coffee consumption in the Western world. Starbucks and Tully's successfully transformed the image of coffee from a home brew to an elegant concoction, and thereby induced us to pay over $2.00 for a simple cup, and up to $4.50 if we wanted it combined with caramel, steamed milk, chocolate, amaretto, whipped cream, and so forth.

My friend, the next time you are tempted to decry the cost of a cup of coffee, I hope you will keep in mind that yours truly once paid $90 for a cup of the stuff. Just the basic brown stuff – a scant 7 ounces in a ceramic cup. Here's how it happened.

As a member of the board of the King County Conservation Voters, I was encouraged to buy a ticket for a fundraising breakfast in downtown Seattle called Wake Up for the Environment. My PAC had reserved a big round table at this somewhat gala annual event sponsored by a sister environmental group. The hope was that at least ten of our board of eighteen would be willing to pay the required $60 per seat and fill up the ten chairs at the table which boasted our name – to show our commitment and dedication.

New to the board this year, I dutifully made the decision to pay the $60 and attend. It would require driving to Seattle in the wee small hours of the morning, as the breakfast was quite early – no one remembered the exact hour – but something like 7:00 AM.

I had reserved a spot earlier but made my payment of $60 over the Internet the night before. I was pretty groggy at the time, as I had arrived home late after a night of teaching at the University of Washington. I took solace in knowing that by prepaying for my breakfast, I wouldn't have to wait in line at the door of the Grand Ballroom at the Westin Hotel.

I also figured that by prepaying I would save some time in the morning – a time cushion in case I had trouble finding a place to park. Indeed, the website said that parking at the hotel was $26.50. Surely I could find a spot cheaper than that, even though it was in downtown Seattle. The website said that registration at the door would begin at 7:15 AM. So, I surmised, the sit-down breakfast must begin at 8:00 AM. I envisioned people mingling, coffee cups in hand, from 7:15 AM till 7:45 AM when they would begin finding their reserved seats, settling in, and nibbling on their fruit cocktails – with the omelets and hot breads arriving around 8:00 AM.

Exhausted from my one-hour drive home on Tuesday night, I fell into bed shortly before midnight after setting the alarm clock for 5:45 AM. I would leave the house about 6:30 AM and arrive in Seattle about 7:15 AM.

Indeed, the morning plan began without too much of a glitch. My husband noted that the radio reported an overturned semi at the on-ramp to I-5. He advised I drive North on local roads and enter I-5 elsewhere. Instead, I decided to leave the house at 6:45 AM, allowing 15 minutes for truck-removal. This slightly delayed departure would still put me at the hotel, I guessed, at 7:30 AM, but mingling with people I don't know for half an hour is not a necessity or even something I can do. Especially before my first cup of coffee.

Rush hour was its usual stop-and-go river of blinking taillights in the predawn darkness, but I arrived at a parking lot across the street from the Westin at 7:45 AM, shortly after sunrise. Granted, this was later than originally planned, but just a quick sprint across the street and I'd be there.

It was one of those parking lots that requires you to push your money into a little slot corresponding to the number painted on the spot where you parked. Ten dollars for the day. Yes, a lot, but less than the $26.50 the hotel would require. I locked up the car and began riffling through my wallet, scrounging up ten dollars in bills. I had it and wouldn't have to raid the visor for emergency money or the ashtray for coins.

A young man in black jeans and a black windbreaker came up and stood a respectful distance as I got my ten ones in a neat little stack and counted them again. "I can take that," he said.

"It's ten, right?" I asked.

"Well, it's actually $14, but ten is close enough." The warning lights started to come on in my brain, but I was in a hurry and befuddled, so I handed him the bills. He began backing away, in a direction away from the shack-like office that served as headquarters for the parking lot.

Sensing something was amiss, I asked with uncertainty, "I don't need to put anything in the box?"

"No," he said. And then he turned and sprinted down the alley, out of sight in an instant.

I noticed a uniformed man, apparently a hotel official, cutting through the lot, heading toward the hotel. I said, "I just paid someone for the parking …"

Before I could finish my sentence, he asked, "Who? Where did he go?"

"A guy in a black jacket," I responded, adding, "He went that way." The official went running off in apparent pursuit of the swindler. Not having time to await the outcome, I returned to my car and found another $10 in bills in my visor. I stuffed this into the box where customers were supposed to pay. So, now I had paid $20 for parking – but still less than hotel parking, I thought as I tried valiantly to rationalize this unfortunate turn of fate. As I crossed the street toward the hotel, I was joined by the official who, while out of breath, said that he had been unable to catch the thief and he was sorry.

Inside the hotel, I found the ballroom was on the fourth floor. I opted for the elevators rather than the escalators, trying to save time. It was almost 8:00 AM now, and I didn't want to disrupt the proceedings. It was possible the speeches would begin as soon as everyone was seated. Outside the ballroom were registration tables, but there was no human traffic now – just a few hosts sitting and quietly chatting. One of them found my name on a list and showed me on a diagram where my table was.

Pushing open the heavy door to the ballroom, I saw that everyone was seated and the speeches were already in process. I promptly found my table and, aha – one empty seat. But when I got to the seat, I found a dirty cloth napkin strewn across it. I lifted it gingerly by one corner, exchanging glances with the man in the next seat whose napkin I assumed it was. He was turned slightly toward me only because that was the direction of the speaker's dais. "Is this yours?" I asked.

"No," he said, looking annoyed. I dropped the napkin and proceeded to sit down, only then noticing that my place setting was not a place setting at all but rather a collection of dirty dishes.

"Is this seat taken?!" I asked, startled.

"Yes, but he's taking pictures. You can sit there." So, I sat down and feigned rapt interest in the speaker. I was absorbing the fact that not only was there no real place for me at the table, but breakfast was over!

"Is breakfast over?" I asked the man next to me.

"Yes, they moved along pretty quickly," he said. *Oh my. This was far from music to my ears.*

Again, I feigned interest in the speakers, clapping dutifully when everyone clapped, and laughing when they laughed. But inside I was crying. I had missed breakfast! And a $60 one at that! No waiter floated up to the table. Of course not. Even if a waiter was still on the floor, he would assume the dirty dishes at my place were mine.

Determined to be a good sport, and knowing I had no one to blame but myself, I tried to take a true interest in the speeches. A speaker was saying, "The goal isn't to get the cars into Seattle during rush hour. The goal is to get the people into Seattle." Amen. I could drink to that. I had just spent over an hour in bumper-to-bumper traffic and had still arrived late. Well, I could drink to that if I had something to drink.

Twisted away from the table to face the speakers, I now turned slightly and cast a furtive glance at what lay upon it. I would kill for a cup of coffee. I saw an insulated coffee pot and – aha! – an empty cup. Corralling these items, I poured the last little bit of coffee into my cup. It was cold and had a few grounds in it, but I gamely added half and half and sugar, pretending nothing was wrong at all. Nothing.

While sipping my tepid inch of coffee, I noticed that at other tables, there were a few muffins and croissants remaining on serving platters. But on our table, nothing. Oh, well, I thought. It was just a continental breakfast. I didn't miss much. But then I noticed something that made my heart sink. A half empty single-serving bottle of ketchup. So, they must have had eggs – probably omelets. My stomach growled reproachfully. "I'm sorry," I murmured.

The man whose seat I had taken, returned for his jacket. He didn't mind that I was in his seat as he was leaving anyway. Well, sure, I would leave, too, now that the food was gone.

The speeches were okay: An award for a man who had pushed through a green building code in the state legislature. And negative comments about Proposition 912 which would repeal the gas tax. Environmentalists believe that gas taxes are good because they cause those who use the roads to pay for them. And they discourage unnecessary use of automobiles.

I do believe in what this breakfast was held for. I do want my children and grandchildren to have access to a comfortable, viable, and efficient system of public transportation. I do believe it is insane that everyone, including me, is propelling tons of steel along concrete every day just to get somewhere. My car is a big container – far too big for just little old me. Why am I depleting resources and polluting the air just to cart around my thrift-shop donations, collections of maps, spare tire, unread newspapers, extra shoes, and so forth? On some level, it is crazy. But then, am I thinking clearly? I haven't yet had my second cup of coffee and none is to be had.

Well, by now you may be wondering about the math. The breakfast was $60, the parking $20. That makes $80, but what about that final $10? I figure the gas for carrying me and my hunk of steel to Seattle and back was another $10 at least. That means I just paid $90 for a cup of coffee.

Trying to salvage the morning, I returned to my car where the hotel official was chatting with the attendant. Oh, sure. Now they had an attendant! The official and I explained to the attendant how I had been robbed. But the management was unmoved and refused to give me even a partial refund.

Well, if I had paid twice for the whole day, I was going to accomplish *something*. I remembered I had a two-year-old Christmas gift in my trunk, a gift of pajamas from Crabtree and Evelyn which I needed to return. A certain relative thought I wore a size Large, but I didn't. And yet, I had never been near the store where I could return these huge PJs. I returned them for store credit, bought some holiday candles and Lily of the Valley soaps with the proceeds, and headed back toward the parking lot. I passed a Tully's and bought a cup of coffee for the road. It cost $2.50. What a bargain!

Bibimbap

Our son, Nick, his wife Chi Hyon, and their four-year-old son Adrian would be spending Christmas with us. For the second year in a row, they would fly to Seattle from Saratoga, California, to join us on this special day. They themselves do not celebrate Christmas at their home. Chi Hyon grew up in Korea as a Buddhist, and Nick has just never been that attached to the traditions of his childhood. But they had decided it would be good for Adrian to be exposed to mainstream American traditions. We had even been given the green light to talk about Santa Claus and have Adrian hang up a stocking, along with leaving snacks for Santa and his reindeer.

The three of them would arrive on the afternoon of December 24th and depart late in the day on December 26th. As grandparents, John and I looked forward to a magical Christmas.

It's long been a tradition for me to make pizza on Christmas Eve. Last year, I added artichoke hearts to the pizza, and was delighted to discover that Chi Hyon loves artichokes. And, although she isn't crazy about many American foods, she does love pizza. One time, when I was making it, she sat at the kitchen island and actually took notes! And when she cooks at their home, I also observe closely and express my appreciation for the dishes she prepares. I learned that Koreans even have a special concept about cooking. They honor the "hand work," a sort of spiritual component that goes into each dish.

A few days before their arrival, John and I watched a TV cooking show that featured Korean food. Brigitte and Julia, of America's Test Kitchen, prepared *bibimbap*. They explained that *bibim* refers to combining a variety of ingredients, and *bap* refers to rice. This popular Korean dish, with deep cultural roots, consists of vegetables, eggs, rice, and a spicy sauce. And, it is typically served with cucumber and bean sprout pickles. The TV chefs made it look easy, so we decided to make it as a late lunch, sort of a snack, after Nick, Chi Hyon, and Adrian arrived on the afternoon of Christmas Eve. I would make pizza later in the evening.

In preparation for making this dish, John and I went to the local Asian food store, H Mart, and bought the rice, chili paste, and toasted sesame seed oil that the recipe called for. It had to be sushi rice, and the chili paste had to be the authentic Korean type.

On the morning of the 24th, we made the pickles, using cucumbers but skipping the bean sprouts which we had been unable to find in the local stores. And, we whipped up the chili sauce. It felt good to be honoring Chi Hyon's Korean culture. After all, she had made amazing efforts to learn about our American culture.

About an hour before heading to the airport to pick up Nick, Chi Hyon, and Adrian, John cooked the rice. He followed the directions precisely, as the texture of the rice was key. It was supposed to be boiled on the stove for exactly seven minutes before being cooled and then pressed into a ceramic Dutch oven for the final browning – key to its yummy success. After just the bottom layer was browned, it would be jumbled up with the unbrowned rice, the sautéed vegetables, and the fried eggs. Then it would be doused with spicy chili sauce.

As the rice simmered in its covered saucepan, I sautéed the carrots, spinach, and shiitake mushrooms.

When the seven minutes were up, John turned off the heat and left the rice to cool, with the lid in place, before he headed for the airport. I stuck the sautéed veggies in the fridge. About an hour later, John arrived home with the precious cargo – Nick, Chi Hyon, and adorable Adrian. Although only four years old, Adrian looked very grown up with his buttoned shirt, V-neck sweater, and even a little-boy tie.

John and I soon were at the stove, ready to whip up the *bibimbap*. Chi Hyon, sliding onto a bar stool on the other side of the kitchen island, seemed pleased that we were trying our hand at a Korean dish. But when we discovered that the rice was still crunchy, we realized we might have been a bit over-ambitious to attempt something new on Christmas Eve. Especially something from another culture.

As we pondered what to do next, Chi Hyon asked, "Why didn't you use the rice cooker?" Indeed, they had given us a rice cooker as a gift several years earlier.

"We use the rice cooker all the time," I said. "But this particular recipe called for a more hands on approach. We wanted to get the texture just right." The TV show had made it look so easy!

"But Caucasians don't know how to cook rice," she said. "That's why we got you a rice cooker." Good point! Not only had she bought us a rice cooker, but she had taken us to a number of Asian restaurants near their home in California. She had helped us gain a new appreciation and respect for rice – its myriad types and textures.

I could understand her frustration; I was frustrated, too. And I could certainly relate to living in a country that prepared food in a way that flew in the face of what one had known and loved since childhood. For example, when John and I had lived in England for a short time, we ate breakfast in a college cafeteria that absolutely destroyed toast – every single morning! What could be so hard about toast? We liked it the American way – hot and crisp. But the Brits had a custom of waving the toast around to cool it off before pounding it with a hammer and then putting the cold flat slabs in a sort of metal coil where any remaining flavor would be promptly dissipated. It had driven us nutty! So, yeah, I could imagine how frustrating it must be to encounter rice that is routinely cooked badly by Americans like me.

Was our *bibimbap* going to be a flop? A *bibimbap* flop? I willed myself to stay calm. It certainly wasn't the first time our forays into cooking had hit a snag. True, it was Christmas, and I wanted everything to be perfect. But this, I realized, was just a blip in the *bibimbap*.

The Christmas tree, twinkling nearby, helped me gain perspective: So, I put my hands into the pockets of my jingle-bell apron and willed each set of fingers to form a Buddhist circle. Like in yoga meditation. With eyes closed, I took a deep breath, allowing the word *namaste* to drift through my mind. I exhaled slowly and opened my eyes.

John was calmly adjusting the flame to get the rice simmering again as Chi Hyon watched with approval. She looked hungry! And who wouldn't be after a three-hour flight with a toddler?! Especially when they don't feed you on planes any more, except for little bags of stale pretzels. She had no doubt turned down this abomination – the most iconic of bland Caucasian snacks. I had often wondered how flight attendants can even live with themselves when distributing such garbage. I could picture them at union meetings, saying, "Okay, we'll pass it out, but no more than five pretzels to a bag. It's just too embarrassing to pretend that this is food!"

Meanwhile, over at the coffee table, Nick and Adrian were building something with Legos while munching on barbeque chips and seaweed.

The rice did get cooked and transferred to the Dutch oven. The bottom browned beautifully, and we then stirred in the sautéed carrots, spinach, and mushrooms. Finally, we added the freshly fried eggs and folded it together with the chili sauce, serving it with additional sauce on the side.

The *bibimbap* was perfect. The fragrance was divine and it was beautiful to look at – the browned rice a nice contrast with the sticky white stuff, the green spinach, the bright orange carrots, and the beige shiitakes. Plus the fried eggs, comfort food by any cultural standard! And the cucumber pickles perched on top. When Chi Hyon spooned up a serving on her plate, she took the time to smile at us and nod with clear approval of our ultimately successful culinary experiment.

I gazed around the table, happy to see that everyone was eating with gusto, especially little Adrian who is a gorgeous composite of chromosomes – both Asian and Caucasian. Later in the evening, our other son, Alex, and his equally diverse family would arrive. We would all eat pizza and then, in the glow of the Christmas tree, help the two young boys, beloved cousins, hang their stockings with care. For the jolly old elf.

This is my family, I thought with deep contentment. My heart was filled with love. It even skipped a beat. I swear it went "bibbity bap."

Speaking Spanish in Cuba

In preparation for our trip to Cuba, I dug up my phrase books and tried valiantly to brush up on the Spanish language. My Spanish was rusty at best, but it did serve me on a handful of occasions during our week-long trip. One example follows.

John and I were in the historic town of Trinidad, located on the Caribbean coast near the Escambray Mountains. We were following our guide over buckling cobblestone streets while enjoying the balmy breezes on this mid-morning excursion. After pointing out a few of the oldest churches and other buildings, he gave us an hour of free time to explore the town on our own.

John and I soon found ourselves on a short street lined with makeshift open-air stalls from which locals sold clothing and handcrafts – little wooden cars, embroidered napkins, hand-stamped leather wallets, and so forth.

One stall sold linen shirts for men. Knowing how much John enjoys these shirts, I urged him to take a look. The Afro-Cuban woman in charge of the stall quickly held up a shirt to John, urging him to try it on. I encouraged him, too. So, John reluctantly pulled the shirt on over his T-shirt. "Too small," he said, seemingly relieved that he'd have an excuse not to shop. The woman, smiling and friendly, indicated that it would fit if it wasn't over his other shirt. She and I, in our respective languages, urged him to take off his T-shirt.

"That's all right," John said. "I really don't need another shirt." He was pulling the linen shirt back over his head. But his T-shirt was going along for the ride.

"Take it off!" we women persisted.

It seemed he had no choice as the T-shirt and linen shirt were coming off in tandem.

Gazing at his naked torso, the woman said, "*Ah! Muy guapo!*"

Knowing this means "Very handsome," I laughed and said, "*Si. Muy guapo. Pero es mio!*"

She immediately got the joke and we laughed together, our eyes linking.

"What did she say?" asked John – amused but confused.

"She said you're very handsome, but I told her you're mine!" Now all three of us were laughing, here in the sunshine, in historic Trinidad, Cuba.

John tried on the shirt again, and it fit so well that he decided to buy it. And, he decided to keep it on and wear it for the rest of the day. It was perfect for the climate.

John proceeded to negotiate the sale with the Cuban money he had on hand. The woman then folded his T-shirt into a bag and handed it to him. Gesturing toward the new linen shirt that he was wearing, she smiled broadly and said once again, "*Muy guapo!*" Then, with a wink at me, she added, "*Pero el es suyo!*" But, he's yours!

I had succeeded in conversing in Spanish. And I believe this went beyond the situations normally addressed in any of my Spanish phrase books!

At The Ocean

John and I were walking along a sandy beach in Mexico, the waves crashing nearby. It was warm but windy, and the ocean sounds made it difficult to carry on a conversation. But I tried: "Do you think they have rogue waves here?" I asked.

"Road rage?!" he asked, incredulous that I would bring this up now of all times.

"No. Rogue waves," I said, laughing.

*   *   *   *

This collection of essays began with my walking up to a lemonade stand and now ends with my walking along an ocean shore. Everywhere, surprises await. I see life as part of an infinite unspooling – mysterious, fragile, and wild. Existential.

Morning Messages

The following three pieces are not essays, but rather the Unitarian-Universalist equivalent of sermons.

It was my pleasure to deliver these at Saltwater Unitarian-Universalist Church in Des Moines, Washington, and subsequently at several other Unitarian churches in the area.

Pete Seeger:
A Life of Singing for Social Justice

Bending Toward Justice:
Birmingham Then and Now

Imagine:
Ground Zero and Strawberry Fields

Pete Seeger: A Life of Singing for Social Justice

Pete Seeger's music has been a part of my life for as far back as I can remember. When I was little, Mom often played Pete and the Weavers on the record player – and my three sisters and I knew almost all the songs by heart.

On May 19, 1958, when I was in eighth grade, Pete Seeger even came to our little town of Yellow Springs, Ohio, to do a concert. I still have the ticket stub which shows that general admission was $1.36 plus .14 tax, for a total of $1.50. Mom piled us four kids into the old Chevy and away we went. On the way, she said excitedly, "I hope he plays 'When the Saints Go Marching In'" – her favorite.

The school auditorium was packed. Pete was wonderful, and we were all singing along with great enthusiasm. But, my sisters and I kept waiting to hear that song Mom especially wanted to hear. Toward the end of the concert, Pete asked for requests and we whispered to Mom, "Request it, request it!" But Mom was very shy, and we were sitting toward the back, so she would have had to speak really loudly.

Hope was fading that Mom could summon up the courage when, luckily, someone else called out that very request. "When the Saints Go Marching In!" And Mom, suddenly exclaimed, "Yeah!" so loudly that everyone could hear!

Then Pete echoed her, "Yeah!" and everyone laughed. We kids were so happy for her. Which is, I think, why I've remembered that moment all these years. As I look back on it now,

I see it as one very personal example of Pete's extraordinary gift for getting everyone to come out of their shells. And for him, it was not just about participation in singing; it was about participation in the broadest possible sense – participation in democracy and in those causes that touch our hearts.

Pete has been like family to me – perhaps like an older brother saying, "Here's something you should pay attention to. Here's something that needs fixing. Let's sing about it and then roll up our shirtsleeves and do something about it."

During my college years, Pete expanded my sense of family to include the family of man, or as we learned to say in the 60s, of humankind. And, still later, he expanded my sense of family to include not just humans, but fish and fowl, and the entire planet and its ecosystem.

Now Pete is almost 93 years old. That's why younger people may not be too familiar with him. But, I hope you will know a bit more about this musical man – a Unitarian – when you leave here today. At the close of my comments this morning, we'll segue to a brief video clip and a beautiful song he wrote in which he addresses his own mortality. But, first let's look at his life.

Pete was born in New York in 1919. His mother was a classical violinist, and his father a music professor. When Pete was old enough, he accompanied his father on field trips into Appalachia and other places where his father was studying folk music. Pete's mother was not into folk music and was rather put off when Pete's instrument of choice turned out not to be the violin, as she had always hoped, but – to her dismay, the banjo.

After Pete's parents divorced, Pete was sent to boarding school. He spent summers on his grandparents' farm, and he loved to wander the fields and forests, developing a bond with nature that later played a huge part in his activism. Like many musicians, he was quiet and introverted. A good student, he later entered Harvard with the goal of becoming a journalist. He was by now pretty good at playing the banjo, but to please his mother, he occasionally attended a chamber music concert.

One night after returning to his dorm from such a concert – classical music – he reflected in his journal about what he felt was missing in such concerts. He wrote, "The audience should be a great chorus." In these words, we can hear his early yearning for a more participatory relationship between audience and performers – an early preference for folk music.

In 1936 college students were avidly discussing what to do about the rise of Hitler. The Communist Party, at that time a legitimate political party in America, wanted the world to quarantine Hitler. The party also supported labor unions and worked to end race discrimination, further attracting Seeger. A person of conscience, Pete decided to join the Young Communist League – an affiliation which, while relatively short-lived, certainly complicated his career in years to come.

More intent on social activism than on his studies, Pete allowed his grades to fall, and had to leave Harvard. He still played the banjo only as a hobby until 1940 when he agreed to play at a New York City benefit for California migrant workers. He later said, "I was a bust. My fingers froze up on me and I forgot words." But he was stunned by the concert's surprise star that night – a relative unknown by the name of Woody Guthrie.

Music historian Alan Lomax says, "You can date the renaissance of American folk song from that night. Pete knew it was his kind of music. It was a pure, genuine fervor, the kind that saves souls."

Guthrie and Pete were soon off on a road trip through Oklahoma and Texas. Together, they bummed meals and jammed with strangers – in backyards and on front porches. Inspired by Guthrie, Seeger next embarked on a solo trip westward, hitchhiking or jumping on freight trains. Playing in saloons, he further cultivated his talent for getting everyone to join in on the choruses. And he truly reveled in hearing the voices of all – the great chorus he had yearned for during that concert at Harvard.

Seeger was in deep sympathy with the labor movement, and he said, "Just as every church has a choir, why not every union?" He, Woody Guthrie, Bess Lomax, Lee Hays, and others formed the singing group, the Almanacs – becoming song leaders of American labor.

In 1941 came Pearl Harbor, and in 1942 Pete was drafted into the army. Meanwhile, he had a sweetheart – Toshi Ohta whose father was a Japanese political refugee. Pete and Toshi married during one of his furloughs. They were so poor that Toshi paid the $2 for their marriage license. From that moment on, she served as Pete's manager and, as he says, his tower of strength.

Toshi had to have a sense of humor to be married to Pete – with his relentless work for liberal causes. She likes to say, teasingly, "If only Peter would chase women instead of chasing causes, I'd have an excuse to leave him." Once, when Pete was being honored, Toshi spoke first. She said, "In my job [Pete's manager], I work 24 hours a day, 7 days a week, 52 weeks a year with no vacation. I [now] want to introduce my husband, Pete – you know, [that] guy who goes around the country singing for the 40-hour week!" The audience just howled.

But, meanwhile, back to the army days. Pete served overseas as a musician, entertaining wounded troops in hospitals. He also played for local children in Saipan and other places. Playing for children remained a favorite activity throughout his life.

After his military tour, Pete and Toshi lived in New York City and started a family. They longed to move to the country. And, although they couldn't afford a house, they did manage to scrape up enough money to buy some land – 17 acres overlooking the Hudson River in upstate New York. Seeger checked out a library book on how to build a log cabin, and almost single-handedly built the modest home in which they raised their children – Dan, Mika, and Tinya. For years they had no electricity or running water, yet they enjoyed, for the most part, being so close to nature.

World War II came to a close, but now we had the Cold War and it was starting to heat up. One of Pete's acquaintances was Paul Robeson – a black scholar, activist, athlete, and singer – credited, among other things, with bringing African-American spirituals to a wider audience. Robeson was also an un-apologetic socialist.

In 1949, Robeson was invited to sing at the Peekskill Resort and asked Seeger to join him. The Ku Klux Klan fanned the flames of local controversy. The concert itself went smoothly, but the aftermath did not. As the Seeger family drove away together, their car, like others, was pelted with rocks by angry protesters. Pete's son, Dan, just a young child at the time, remembers his grandfather Takashi, pushing him and his sister onto the floor of the car to protect them from the flying glass. This harrowing experience deeply affected Pete. He vowed to keep his family safe but also resolved to continue peacefully expressing his values through music.

Meanwhile, Pete had joined a quartet called the Weavers. This talented group soon had two hits at the top of the charts

–"Tzena Tzena" and "Good Night, Irene." But Seeger was uncomfortable with commercial success. So, when the Weavers were put up in fancy hotels, he would stay with friends or in cheap rooming houses.

In 1952, the proverbial hammer fell, and Seeger was called up by the House Un-American Activities Committee (HUAC), citing his past association with the Communist Party and his social activism. Seeger was calm and respectful – but he refused to sign a loyalty oath. He said he resented the implication that he was un-American just because his opinions might be different from members of the Congressional committee.

Pete was willing to go to jail, if necessary, in support of his belief that in the United States, people can freely hold and express their own opinions – and should never be required to sign a loyalty oath.

Pete also goes down in history as the first and only person to show up at a congressional hearing with a banjo. At one point, he was grilled about having sung the song, "Wasn't That a Time," a song some Congressmen considered subversive. Seeger said he considered the song deeply patriotic, and offered to play and sing it, as evidence.

The House Un-American Activities Committee was not amused. Instead of allowing him to play, they convicted him of contempt of Congress for his refusal to sign the oath. The conviction was repealed after seven years and some years later, Seeger was even awarded a Congressional Living Legend Award. Pete said of the era of blacklisting, "I really believed, and I think I was right, that in the long run this country doesn't go in for things like that."

Not long after this ordeal, the Weavers performed at Carnegie Hall – to a sell-out crowd that felt that the House Un-American Activities Committee was, in itself, un-American. Despite this affirmation by fans, Pete didn't stay with the Weavers. The group had become too commercial for him, and he decided it was time to part ways.

Although Seeger was officially vindicated, he was one of many artists harmed by what is now generally known as the McCarthy era. Folk music was extremely popular in the 60s, with musicians like Woody and Arlo Guthrie, Joan Baez, Bob Dylan, and Peter, Paul, and Mary, singing their hearts out at hootenannies and on television.

Meanwhile, Seeger was banned from television for 17 years for his refusal to sign that loyalty oath. But he was well-received on college campuses. He said "People are searching for roots in a world of change." Pete offered these roots – this historic connection – telling the stories and struggles of the American people through their music – folk music.

In 1957, at a civil rights event, Pete sang a relatively obscure song, "We Shall Overcome." Martin Luther King was there and liked the song. It soon rose to play a central role in the movement. Pete did not write the song, but changed the words from "we will overcome" to "we shall overcome." Why? Because he noticed that when you say the word, "shall," you can't help but smile. He also added the verse, "We'll walk hand in hand."

Pete participated in countless marches and rallies, and he and Toshi marched proudly in the famous Selma march – a perilous three-day march in which songs provided a constant source of courage and resolve. Seeger said, "I don't think there was any movement in history that had as much singing as the civil rights movement." He added, "Music is not just a distraction. Some music helps you understand your troubles, and some music helps you do something about them."

There was a sobering event in the 70s when a Vietnam vet met with Seeger backstage, after a concert. The former soldier had been outraged that Seeger wanted the U.S. to pull out of the war. But, during the concert, Seeger's songs had moved him. So, after the concert, the man came backstage and asked to speak with Seeger. Toshi arranged for the two to sit down together. The man said, "Mr. Seeger, I came to kill you tonight." He went on to explain that he had lost friends in the war. He was upset and confused, but Pete's songs had dispelled his anger. As they sat together, Pete picked up his banjo and began singing, "Where Have All the Flowers Gone." The former soldier wept.

The Seeger family's property overlooked the Hudson River which in 1967 was horribly polluted. With help, Seeger built and launched the majestic sloop Clearwater which in turn launched a whole era of people working to clean up the Hudson. For decades now, school kids have gone out on this boat to learn about ecology firsthand. Says Pete, "The kids go back to school – and some of them have had their lives changed." The annual Clearwater Festivals have inspired river clean-ups throughout the country.

Recently, I heard Pete on the Tavis Smiley (radio) Show, sharing a special memory about a 1969 peace demonstration in Washington, D.C. He recalled trying to get everyone to sing together, but with 500,000 that was hard. By the time the voices of those in the back reached the front, those in the front were on a different lyric. Pete decided to lead the crowd in a slow and simple song – John Lennon and Yoko Ono's, "Give Peace a Chance."

"Well," said Pete settling into the memory, "You know, Peter, Paul, and Mary jumped up on the stand and started singing it with me. Mitch Miller of 'Sing Along with Mitch' - he jumped up and started waving his arms. After a minute or so, 10,000 people were singing along. After two or three minutes, like 100,000 were singing along. After five or six minutes, all 500,000 were singing it over and over." *All we are saying is give peace a chance*.

Choking up with emotion, Pete continued sharing his memory of this event: "And parents would put their children up on their shoulders so they could see, and the whole crowd like a gigantic ballet was swaying from right to left, slowly, and then back." He concluded, "It was one of the most moving experiences I've ever had in my life."

Yes, for Pete Seeger it has always been about participation. When we participate, we feel our connection to one another. And when we sing, this connection becomes palpable. Thank you, Pete, for all you have done for social justice. We'll treasure the old songs, write some new ones, and always add our voices to the chorus.

Note: At the close of this "Morning Message," we projected on the screen a video of Pete Seeger singing a song he wrote.

"To My Old Brown Earth"
To my old brown earth
and to my old blue sky
I'll now give these last few molecules of "I."

And you who sing,
And you who stand nearby,
I do charge you not to cry.

Guard well our human chain,
Watch well you keep it strong,
As long as sun will shine.

And this our home,
Keep pure and sweet and green,
For now I'm yours
And you are also mine.

Note: Pete Seeger and his wife, Toshi, wcre both alive when I wrote and delivered this Morning Message at several Unitarian churches. However, Toshi Seeger died on July 9, 2013, at the age of 91. Pete Seeger died on January 27, 2014, at the age of 94. He outlived Toshi by only about six months.

Bending Toward Justice:
Birmingham Then and Now

Birmingham, Alabama, was the city in the deep South that in 1963 Martin Luther King, Jr., referred to as "probably the most thoroughly segregated city in the United States." At two separate times in my life, I lived in Birmingham – first when I was in high school. And later, in 1967, when I returned for three months as a civil rights worker.

Before our move to Alabama in 1958, our family of six was living in Yellow Springs, Ohio, where my father was a professor at Antioch College. Rather suddenly his research agenda led to work at the University of Alabama Medical Center, and before you could say Ulysses S. Grant, we found ourselves living in the deep South.

I was a teenager and fitting into teenage culture is always hard. Actually, our entire family had a hard time fitting in. We talked and dressed funny, we held unpopular views, and we attended the Unitarian Church, known for its liberal, progressive beliefs. Each welcoming neighbor would almost immediately ask what church we went to. When we responded, "Unitarian," the inevitable response was, "Isn't that the church in the woods near the zoo?" It was.

Actually, it was a blessing to be near the zoo. On those Sunday mornings when the church received bomb threats, we could quickly escort the Sunday school classes across the street for an impromptu field trip. Why bomb threats? Because many in the church criticized Governor George Wallace while actively supporting integration.

My parents, my three sisters, and I were all dismayed to see the 'white only' signs over drinking fountains and at the entrance to swimming pools and parks. When we went to movies, we watched the black children filing up to the balcony – the only place they were allowed to sit. Although I was white, I found it frightening. In Ohio, my best friend, Sandra Anderson, happened to be African-American. Her father, Walter Anderson, was the chair of Antioch's music department. Although Walter taught a few children, he mostly worked with college students, including Coretta Scott who later became Coretta Scott King.

When Coretta, an education major, needed to fulfill her student-teaching requirement, the Yellow Springs public schools refused to accommodate her. She was able to fulfill her requirement through a patchwork of teaching positions. My mother ran a small nursery school in our home, and she offered Coretta a position there. My point is that the race thing for me is personal.

Although I was too young to remember Coretta, I do remember Sandra who is still a close friend. As kids, we had played jump rope and hopscotch together, and prowled the campus where both our fathers taught. At our progressive elementary school, we played a version of hide-and-go-seek that we called "underground railroad." Indeed, our small Ohio town had been an important link in the underground railroad a century earlier.

But, back to Alabama. As soon as I graduated from high school, I returned to Ohio, becoming a freshman at Antioch in 1962. The following year, efforts to integrate Birmingham went into high gear. With the leadership of Reverend Martin Luther

King, Jr., African-Americans began peacefully claiming their rights. But the response, as we know, was not peaceful. Reverend King was jailed in April of 1963, and it was then that he wrote his famous *Letter from the Birmingham Jail*. This included the familiar passage, "We are caught in an inescapable network of mutuality, tied in a single garment of destiny. Whatever affects one directly affects all indirectly. Never again can we afford to live with the narrow, provincial 'outside agitator' idea."

A couple months after Reverend King was released from jail, Governor Wallace blocked the door of the University of Alabama, attempting to prevent two black students from enrolling. In September, President John Kennedy federalized the National Guard to insure the peaceful integration of two public schools.

Five days later, the 16th Street Baptist Church was bombed and four young girls were killed. Two months after that, in November, John Kennedy was assassinated in Dallas. All this happened in 1963 when Sandra and I were college sophomores, studying at Ohio colleges a few hours apart.

Many of us coming of age at this time were stunned and frightened about the violence against those working peacefully for change. At the same time, thousands, millions, of people, regardless of race, were in awe of the emergence of Martin Luther King and his principle of nonviolence.

I'd like to also credit a relatively unsung hero – a Unitarian minister who gave a sermon in 1853 that Reverend King drew upon in some of his speeches. This Unitarian minister was Reverend Theodore Parker who, like King, not only talked the talk but walked the walk. Before the emancipation of slaves, Reverend Parker took personal risk in breaking the law and sheltering runaway slaves in his Boston home. He died shortly before the Civil War, not living to see emancipation or even the election of Abraham Lincoln.

But before Reverend Parker died, in an 1853 sermon he proclaimed his moral philosophy in words later echoed by Martin Luther King, and more recently by President Barack Obama. He said: "Look at the facts of the world. You see a continual and progressive triumph of [what is morally] right. I do not pretend to understand the moral universe; the arc is a long one."

Parker continued, "My eye reaches but little ways; I cannot calculate the curve – by the experience of sight; I can divine it by conscience. And from what I see, I am sure it bends towards justice."

Reverend King read Reverend Parker's sermons in seminary and found the concept of the moral arc to be a powerful one. He carried it forward while distilling it into a single sentence: "The arc of the moral universe is long but it bends towards justice." In a few minutes I'll share how President Obama has also built on the legacy of this concept.

But, for now, I want to return to my own small story within this huge, centuries-long, American struggle. In 1965, a small group of students and recent graduates from Harvard Law School went to Montgomery, Alabama, and founded *The Southern Courier*, a newspaper with the goal of providing balanced coverage of the civil rights movement.

In winter of '67, *The Courier* needed a reporter to cover Birmingham. Still at college in Ohio, I needed a work-study position for that quarter, so I was soon off to Montgomery on a Greyhound Bus. There I was issued a car and a camera and sent on to Birmingham.

One morning, I read a one-inch report buried in the back pages of the *The Birmingham News*. A black man had been spotted running near a school where, in the past, they claimed break-ins had been attempted. The report said that the police yelled *Stop!* and then fired a warning shot into the air. Later they found the body of 18-year-old James Small. That was how *The Birmingham News* reported it.

The officers apparently needed only to express mild surprise that a shot fired into the air could somehow lodge squarely in someone's back. In Birmingham, in those days, a police report like this was not questioned by the authorities. No official investigation would ensue. This was the type of investigating that fell to reporters from *The Southern Courier.*

I made my way to the police station to request the official report. While waiting for a clerk to retrieve the file from a back room, I adopted a nonchalant attitude in front of the police officer in charge. Another officer, on other business, strode into the building, the door slamming behind him. His hand was bandaged.

"What happened to you?" asked a policeman who was milling about – quickly adding in jocular tones, "Didn't I tell you never to hit a Negro in the head?!" But he didn't say "Negro." The officers – all white, of course – laughed. A black couple sat waiting for something, keeping their eyes lowered.

"What business is this matter to you, little lady?" the officer in charge now asked. I said I was a reporter for *The Southern Courier,* and fortunately he didn't appear to have heard of it. He handed me the report, and I read that Officer R.G. Haltom had fired "to apprehend a fleeing felon." Hmmn. Not exactly how it was reported in *The Birmingham News*. I wondered just where the cover-up had begun. What evidence did they have that he

131

was a felon? No break in had occurred that night, nor – I later learned – in the past.

After my visit to the police station, I knew I needed to meet with James' family to get their side of the story. I enlisted the help of a friend of mine from high school. Joyce had been raised to be an elitist Southern lady, but she had rebelled against her own culture. She still dressed in pastel and had every blond hair in place. Yet she was well aware of Birmingham's racist policies, and events like this angered her. She was an important ally and knew her way around the city far better than I.

We located the Smalls' home and soon sat in their living room where grief hung heavily in the air. Charlena, the sister, said that James had gotten home late after a date and the two of them were talking late into the night. Maybe, as people their age are apt to do, they were constructing dreams for the future or solving the world's problems.

Around 1:30 AM, they ran out of cigarettes and Charlena convinced James to go buy some from a machine at a nearby gas station. It was not wise for a young black man to be on the streets late at night. But, teenagers are not known for always using good judgment.

When James did not return promptly, Charlena eventually fell asleep on the sofa.

Early the next morning, Mrs. Small said she was awakened by a phone call: "Do you have a son named James Small?"

"Yes, sir."

"Well, you better come get him 'cause he's in the morgue."

As Mrs. Small shared this story with us, she sat on her sofa, weeping. Charlena tried to comfort her and then told us that when they went to identify the body, they were handed James's effects – simply his hat, his money clip, and a fresh unopened pack of cigarettes. They learned that James was killed just two blocks from his home. Mrs. Small, clearly heartbroken, said that she was active in the movement and couldn't help wondering if this was some kind of retaliation.

Dr. King had said in his *Letter from the Birmingham Jail* that in any nonviolent campaign the first step is the collection of facts. So Joyce and I went to the funeral home to find out the truth about how James died.

The funeral would be the following day, so today the funeral home was empty but for the two of us, the friendly black proprietor, and James Small. The proprietor knew we were here to ascertain the location of the bullet that killed this young man. James had clearly been a strong and healthy young man in the prime of his life. The proprietor showed us exactly where the bullet had entered his back. The "warning shot."

Joyce and I exchanged looks with the proprietor and the three of us shook our heads in sorrow. After thanking the proprietor, we stepped back outside into the harsh February sunlight.

Later that day, I filed my report with *The Southern Courier* and it was soon front page news in that Montgomery-based newspaper.

A few evenings later, I went to a meeting at a black Baptist church where Reverend Fred Shuttlesworth, of the Southern Christian Leadership Conference (SCLC), spoke. "Every time you turn around, some Negro's being killed by some trigger happy policeman in Birmingham," he said. "Every time one of your sons is accused of some crime, some policeman's bullets serve as judge, jury, and courts."

Indeed, there had been 14 killings in 12 months. He invited the Smalls to come up and tell their story. Still overcome with grief, they asked if I would speak for them. I was extremely shy at the time, but something about that pack of cigarettes spoke of a tragic truth that needed telling. So I made my way up to the pulpit and told the story of James Small.

And now I have shared this story with you. I feel it's important to tell this story because it represents thousands of casualties of the civil rights movement – African-Americans who were shot, lynched, beaten, jailed, or attacked by police dogs. It's incredible that in the face of scorn, hatred, and violence, blacks in the South continued to demonstrate peacefully for their rights. One thing I learned is that much of their courage and resolve was born and nurtured in their churches.

Much has changed. Not enough – but much has changed. Who could have even dreamed at that time – in 1967 – that a few decades later our country would elect a black President. On election night 2007, many of us gathered with friends to watch Barack Obama accept his position as our president-elect.

As President-Elect Obama made his way to the front of the stage, he walked in measured steps as if aware that his steps were made possible by earlier steps – the weary steps of maids and gardeners in Montgomery, Alabama, walking for miles on tired feet to get to work during the bus boycott, the steps of protesters crossing a bridge in Selma as they faced police dogs, heavily-armed officers on horseback, tear gas, and rocks from jeering crowds. And other steps: Steps of school children facing fire hoses and fists as they simply exercised their consti-tutional right to demonstrate, the steps of Rev. King, climbing to a podium to speak to thousands, gathered at the Lincoln Memorial in our nation's capital.

Obama said, "If there is anyone out there who still doubts that America is a place where all things are possible; who still wonders if the dream of our founders is alive in our time; who still questions the power of our democracy, tonight is your answer." Obama gave his acceptance speech at Grant Park, the same Chicago park that had seen violent confrontations between anti-war demonstrators and police during the 1968 Democratic Convention. Then, this park had been the site of animosity, violence, and despair. Now, it hosted a rainbow crowd in the throes of peaceful jubilation.

President Obama's road has been rocky. But he appears to have the same visionary stance as Reverend Parker and Martin Luther King. One of my favorite quotes of his is, "Let us not be defined by our differences, but by what we share in common." And, Obama has built on the legacy of Parker's vision of the moral arc by saying, "The arc doesn't bend on its own. It bends because we put our hands on it and bend it in the direction of justice."

The Smalls, now all deceased, were ordinary people living in extraordinary times. They lived with dignity and they practiced nonviolence. I'm sure that Mrs. Small's fight for civil rights was, in part, a fight for the future of her children. Yet it was other children, not hers, who ultimately benefitted from her sacrifice and the sacrifice of so many like her.

For example, consider a child named Annetta Watts, born in 1959 to a nurse and her coal-miner husband in Birmingham. Annetta was only four years old when Dr. King wrote that famous letter – and when that bomb went off in church. She was seven when James Small was shot in her city and eight when Dr. King was assassinated. Most likely, she heard talk of these events both at home and at church.

Years later, with the governor no longer blocking the entrance, Annetta was able to attend the University of Alabama. In 2003, Annetta Watts Nunn became the first woman, and the second African American, to be named Chief of Police of the City of Birmingham. She noted on the city website that the police were committed to serving everyone with dignity and respect. No longer are racist jokes told in the station lobby by an all-white police force.

And consider another child – the daughter of Governor George Wallace. Peggy Wallace Kennedy spoke not long ago of the marchers in Selma, saying, "I knew in my heart that their cause was just, but unlike them I did not let my voice be heard." She, the daughter of a segregationist icon, supported the candidacy of an African-American to be president of the United States. This shows how far we've moved along the moral arc of the universe – toward justice.

My friend Sandra and I still keep in touch. About the only disagreement we've had was during Obama's first campaign. She supported Hillary Clinton, and I – supported someone else. She's writing her memoirs now. Almost every week, I get another installment from her. When we were about eight years old, we pricked our fingers and pressed them together to be blood sisters. And, to this day, we sign our letters, "Your sister."

Well, even if you're not writing your memoirs, I encourage those of you who have seen positive change in the world to talk about the way things were – and how far we've come. Talk about the way that hard times in our country have inspired people to summon strength they didn't know they had and to join with others in working for social justice.

When you see things that need changing, remember the people of Birmingham, and others, who dared to dream of change and peacefully work for it despite huge, frightening, and even deadly obstacles. As Police Chief Watts said, "The Movement was led by members of the faith community who came outside the walls of their places of worship to change not only our community, but the world." There is still much work to be done, much that needs changing. Let us continue this work, moving ever-forward on the moral arc toward justice.

Note: A few years after I wrote this morning message, there were some high-profile cases of police shootings of black people. I realized, with sorrow, that this sermon was overly optimistic. Whites are finally beginning to acknowledge what blacks have known all along: institutionalized racism still exists in police departments across the country. At least now, investigations occur, so these killings can no longer be hidden from public scrutiny. Still, it is a shameful reality that black people still are not safe from these terrible injustices and brutalities. *Black lives matter.*

Imagine: Ground Zero and Strawberry Fields

It was a hot August afternoon in New York City. My husband John and I were ensconced in a rickshaw, being transported comfortably through Central Park by a young man pedaling a sturdy bike attached to the rickshaw. We normally refrain from touristy things like this. But, the young man needed customers, and he won us over. As we had settled into the comfortable and colorful rickshaw, our driver had begun pedaling vigorously. Then, twisting his wiry body and speaking in broken English, he told us his name was Yuri and that he was from Nevsehir, a small town in Turkey. He was here on a student visa, and this job enabled him to work on his English.

This special journey started at the southern end of the park where we told Yuri we just wanted to go northward, in the general direction of our hotel on the upper west side. "But we definitely want to see Strawberry Fields," said John.

"And get out and spend some time there," I added.

"Have you seen Strawberry Fields before?" he asked.

"No, but we're John Lennon fans."

"Do you know about this?" he asked.

"No, not really." We had not been to New York City since 1984, and then only passing through. I had lived in NYC in the late 60s and early 70s before moving to Washington, D.C., and meeting John. In New York, I had been at Bank Street College of Education – first as a graduate student and then as a Head

Start and Follow Through Teacher-Trainer. Being back in New York after all these years had elements of *déjà vu*. So much the same, yet so much had changed.

Back to the rickshaw. Despite our jet lag, we leaned forward to better hear Yuri's spiel about the Strawberry Fields part of the park – our destination. Yuri said, "Strawberry Fields was dedicated in 1985 by Yoko Ono, five years after the death of John Lennon. There is a mosaic there made of black and white tiles, a gift of Naples, Italy. Strawberry Fields is a Lennon song he wrote when remembering an orphanage by that name near the house in Liverpool where he grew up. It has all new landscaping, with 161 species of plants – gifts from many nations of the United Nations."

As we absorbed this information, Yuri returned his full attention to pedaling. We leaned back and let the summer breeze flow over us as we jounced along. Starting the next day, I would be secluded in classrooms at Columbia, attending an educational conference. So, John and I had already spent much of this day – a Sunday – taking in many of New York's attractions. Tired, we relaxed into the padded recesses of the rickshaw cabin, gazing at the canopy of green branches above.

As we headed up a hill, the rickshaw slowed to a crawl. Yuri said, "Very steep, sorry." He began traversing to reduce the grade, standing up as he pedaled, panting, swerving. John said, "If you want, we can get out. And even push."

We were just about to do that when suddenly we felt the rickshaw rocket forward from some mysterious new force. A large hand off to our left had grabbed the side of our cabin and was pushing, propelling the rickshaw up the hill. Enclosed in our cabin, we couldn't yet see the owner of this hand, but it was a person whose dark skin was made even darker by tattoos. We were amazed and delighted to be the recipients of this sudden and well-timed helping hand. Soon, we could see handlebars and a bicycle wheel off to our left and discern that another rickshaw driver was lending his strength to the task of getting our rickshaw up the hill.

"Thank you," said Yuri, gratefully.

"No problem," said the other young man. Now we could see him, as he had pulled up a little closer. "This hill can be tough," he added with a friendly smile. And so, in this manner, the two bicyclists – the Turkish student and the good Samaritan, carried us – two weary aging hippies – up the hill to Strawberry Fields.

The central plaza of Strawberry Fields could be reached only by foot, so at a certain point, we disembarked, agreeing to meet Yuri on the other side, near Central Park West. We made our way up a quiet path, arriving at a small plaza in the center of which was the simple black-and-white mosaic honoring the memory of John Lennon.

Here we joined a dozen or so others who stood quietly gazing at the round mosaic which had, in its center, the single word "Imagine." This song had always been a favorite of mine: "Imagine all the people, Living life in peace. You may say I'm a dreamer, But I'm not the only one. I hope someday you will join us, And the world will be as one."

The cluster of tourists wordlessly self-organized – taking turns to have their picture taken next to the simple seven-letter word now immortalized not only in song but in stone. *IMAGINE*. Walking on, we encountered a group of older musicians singing the Lennon/McCartney song "In My Life": "There are places I remember, All my life, though some have changed, Some have gone and some remain."

The lyrics brought tears to my eyes and prompted me to place a few bills in the guitar case sitting open on the pavement. The musicians – gray-haired and balding – nodded and smiled. I had a sense that we were acknowledging a shared past – not just living through the 60s, but remembering it with fondness.

We met Yuri where the park meets Central Park West. As we climbed back into the rickshaw, he pointed across the street to the Dakota, the residential hotel where Yoko and John had lived and where Yoko still lives part of the year. My gaze fell on the entryway where Lennon had been shot. Yuri pointed out the windows on the penthouse apartment facing the park as well as a high window to the room where the white piano was, where Lennon had composed "Imagine."

Back in the late 60s and early 70s, when I lived in New York, the city was a place of tension. My peers and I had participated in protest marches against the war and for civil rights. I remember in particular the spontaneous march just hours after those students were shot at Kent State. Despite the hectic times, I still had my job to do. Almost every day, I descended into the subway and headed for the projects – in Manhattan, Brooklyn, or the Bronx.

In all these boroughs, I worked in Head Start daycare centers with dedicated teaching teams. It seemed there was so much in the city, the country, and the world that needed to be fixed. But, the sixties were also a time of great optimism. We shared a belief that our work mattered and that change was possible. I still believe this, and our trip to New York City provided some welcome proof.

Earlier on this day, this rickshaw day, our first in the city, we had headed for Ground Zero – the site of the former World Trade Center buildings. While crossing Broadway on the upper west side, en route to the subway, we were temporarily stranded on the median strip. This gave us time to admire the lush garden growing right there on the median. A sign credited this pocket garden to a nearby store, in collaboration with the Parks Department. This was certainly different from the bare-dirt median strips I remembered from my earlier days in New York.

Throughout our trip, we noticed hundreds of little flower gardens, nestled in nooks and crannies. Often they were enclosed by little ornamental fences – pragmatic, but mostly symbolic – as if to say, "Someone is tending to this little plot of earth. Please enjoy and respect it." Those who tended these petite gardens had clearly risen above cynicism and instead put their faith in the good will of the people who shared their communities.

The subway tunnels were still noisy and, at this time of year, hot. But they were now free of graffiti. As a crowded train pulled into the station, we were among the last to board, and we faced the closing door dilemma – to push our way in or just wait for the next train. But a passenger already on board held the closing door open till we were safely aboard. Again, like the good Samaritan in the park, a helping hand just when we needed one.

A bit later, leaving the subway tunnel, we found ourselves amid a pilgrimage of tourists looking for the empty place where once the twin towers had stood. When I first caught site of the open area, encircled by a tall fence, my throat tightened and tears welled up. Everyone fell silent in this strange zone – a place we had seen on TV but never in person. Beyond the huge fence, we could see the towering orange cranes, most of them unmanned on this Sunday, but a couple of them moving slowly, doing some sort of catch up in the daunting, complex task of building something new here, something that would honor the memory of all those who died.

Across the street from the World Trade Center site, on one side, we saw a very old cemetery – one with those thin, flat stones, standing crookedly like dominoes about to topple. Near the entrance to this cemetery, several vendors were selling photograph books about 9/11. I bought one, and we retreated into the cemetery to look at it and catch our breath.

John pointed out that we were standing at the very spot where one of the photos was taken. There was that gravestone, there was that tree. They appeared identical in both the photo and in the reality of where we stood. But in the photo, the ground was littered with debris and dust from the newly-collapsed buildings just across the narrow downtown street. Today, the cemetery grass was green and the tree sported shiny new leaves.

In the seven days that we spent in New York City, I wondered how much of the good will we experienced might have been a direct result of this tragedy. Perhaps a tragedy like that reminds people that "We're all in this together." And we can prove that people are still basically good.

One hot afternoon, heading back to the hotel after a day at Columbia, I was overcome by thirst and stopped at a street kiosk that sold snacks, newspapers, and water. I spotted the proprietor, an elderly man, looking wilted from the heat. He pointed to the cooler and when I had the icy bottle in hand, he signaled for me to give cooler door an extra push to make sure it was closed all the way. He grinned a toothless grin when my extra push apparently did the trick, saving him the trouble of leaving his shady enclosure. Well, of course, I was happy to give the heavy cooler door that extra push.

It seemed to me that these little acts somehow characterized present-day New York City. Nothing extraordinary, just small moments of caring – whether pushing a rickshaw up a hill, pushing a subway door open, or pushing a refrigerator door closed on a sweltering summer day. We've all heard of death by a thousand cuts. What seemed to be at work in New York now was life by a thousand acts of random kindness. No one act heroic – and yet all these little acts adding up to something good – a sense of civic community, of caring for other people, other creatures, and the environment.

New York City is not unique. These kindnesses occur every-where. I think it's just that when traveling, one is especially dependent on the kindness of strangers. And, the traveler has special opportunities to honor and participate in these affirming rituals.

One night in our hotel, we watched a special called *The Human Spark*. This presented research about helpfulness. They showed experiments demonstrating the apparently inborn tendency of even toddlers to help others – for example in trying to reach something out of range.

It was shown that even chimps have evolved with this instinct to help another primate reach something. But there the similarity ends. Humans have evolved further. Even toddlers are able, and willing, to volunteer help to others in increasingly complex ways. And, we humans of all ages seem to derive pleasure from helping others. It goes beyond teaching – it is apparently in our DNA.

This spirit of helpfulness characterized our visit – A heavily tattooed fellow-passenger on the subway telling us our stop was next, a taxi driver, in turban, asking which train we were taking from Penn Station, so he could take us to the best possible door.

A female police officer offering us advice on how best to get around an area cordoned off for a Dominican Republic parade. Someone at the Museum of Modern Art telling us which café had the shortest lines. We rarely had to even ask for help because it was so forthcoming!

One morning, we had breakfast at Tom's Restaurant on the corner of 112th and Broadway – my coffee shop from over 30 years ago when my office was nearby. As the waitress poured our coffee, she was singing. "Ah! You're singing!" I said with appreciation.

"Yes, every day," she said, smiling. Walking away with the steaming pot, she added in her Greek accent, "Every day! Every day I sing!"

All this good will came to a crescendo on our last night there. We had gone to see "The Jersey Boys," a feel-good musical about Frankie Valli and the Four Seasons. We emerged on Broadway with the music of Frankie Valli still ringing in our ears: "Oh, What a Night" and "Sherry, Sherry baby, Sherry can you come out tonight?"

Well, it was quite a night! And Sherry baby probably was out tonight – along with everyone else in New York City. The streets were filled, everyone enjoying the gentle breeze and easy camaraderie. We headed toward Times Square and were impressed by the panoply of huge digital displays stacked high into the sky like children's blocks. They bathed a spacious walking mall with warm light.

Families of tourists posed and took photos of each other with small cameras or cell phones. Some were enjoying hot dogs or other goodies from food carts. Young couples walked hand in hand. A little girl rode high on her father's shoulders. A little boy shared fist bumps with a police officer. A family of tourists, speaking Spanish, took pictures of each other. I offered to take their photo together and they smiled, handed me their camera, and assembled themselves – "*Uno, dos, tres, whiskey!*"

I had to admit that these LCD screens were not ecological. Still, at that moment I felt something in the air – what to me was an undeniable celebration of democracy, New York City, rebirth, and diversity. It was as if fireworks were suspended in mid-air, brilliant in the night sky.

Groups of tourists perched on a nearby set of bleachers, taking in the panoramic view. We, too, climbed up and sat awhile, drinking in the atmosphere. I said to John, "It's so peaceful!" I sensed that this city had achieved a new normal. After the seismic changes of the 60s and 70s, and even the tragedy of 9/11, the city was okay. In some ways better than ever. It was a strong reminder that people can get along. And that we're still working out this experiment of being humans together.

Then, my eye was drawn to a huge LCD screen depicting people of all ages and ethnicities dancing – all facing the same way and moving their arms and legs in comical ways – much the way monkeys or children might dance – with elbows and knees poking out. Below each clip the name of the location appeared: Mumbai, India; Stone Town, Zanzibar; Teotihuacan, Mexico; San Paulo, Brazil. A clip with the caption, "Israel" was followed by a clip of Palestine.

Every cluster of dancers included the same guy, Matt Harding – now famous for, as he says, "dancing badly around the world." In his travels, he set the conditions for these spontaneous local dances, resulting in a U-Tube video called "Where the hell is Matt." It was the perfect video for that moment because it so captured and celebrated our common humanity.

I know problems still exist and that if we had stayed in New York longer, we would have experienced some disappointments as well as what I've described here. And, my husband points out that it isn't just New York City that has survived and matured, but me. Still, the fact remains that we humans are still working out ways to live in peace. In New York, I was reminded that we can imagine it, create it and experience it – even if just in pockets of time and space.

In this holiday season, and in the coming year, may we find peace and joy with our friends, our families, and even among strangers and fellow-travelers. We are all in this together – all of us on this wondrous planet. And now, please enjoy the dancing video that we, and hundreds of others, watched that night right in the heart – the core – of the Big Apple.

Note: The video "Where the Hell is Matt?" can be found on You Tube. The following link may help:

https://www.youtube.com/watch?v=zlfKdbWwruY

This silly yet profound video always bring tears to my eyes and gives me hope for the future of the human species and for life on planet earth.

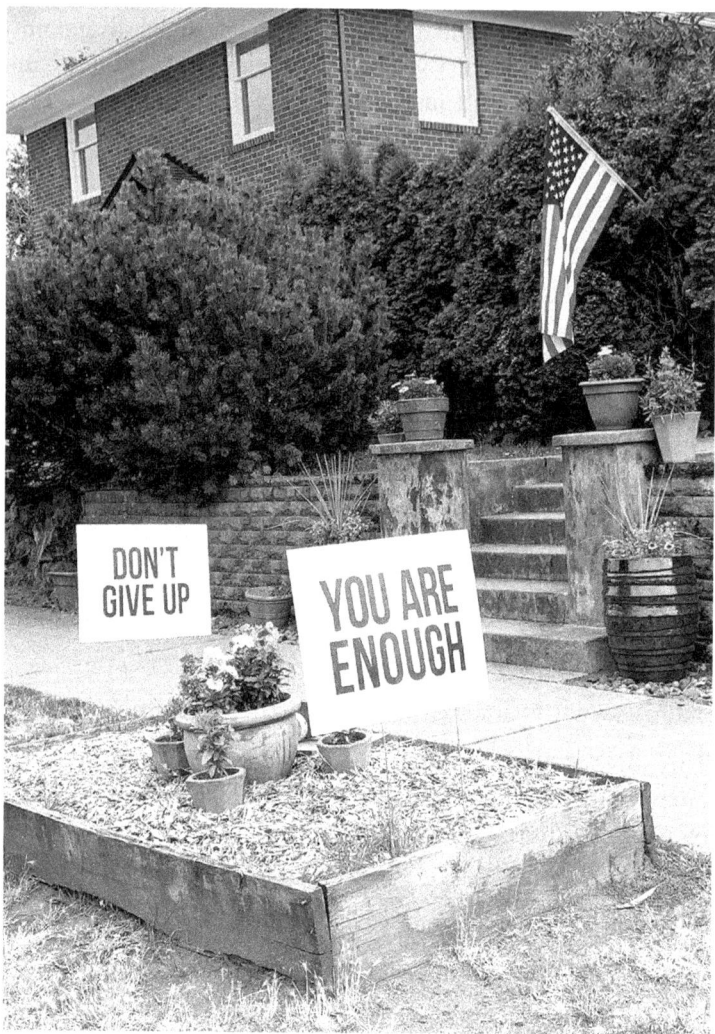

(A drive-by "soothing" seen in Queen Anne, Seattle)

About the Author

Joan Tornow was born in Rochester, New York, and moved to Yellow Springs, Ohio, as a child. In the seventh grade, she and her family moved to Birmingham, Alabama, where she attended high school. She returned to Ohio for college at Antioch where she earned an B.A. in Literature.

Joan then attended Bank Street College of Education in New York City, receiving a M.S. in Early Childhood Education. She worked as an educational consultant for Bank Street College, taking part in the Head Start and Follow Through programs.

Joan later married John Tornow, and they had two sons. They lived in Washington, D.C.; Denver, Colorado; Stoke on Trent, England; Camp Springs, Maryland; Marysville, California; Durham, New Hampshire; Geilenkirchen, Germany; Austin, Texas; and Seattle, Washington.

While living in Austin, Texas, Joan received a Ph.D. in Education, specializing in Literacy Studies. She also published *Link/Age: Composing in the Online Classroom* (Utah State University Press). After this, Joan pursued a career as a memoir instructor and coach.

Joan likes taking photographs, walking her dog, playing the piano, cooking, and writing. Her favorite pastime is hanging out with husband, John, and grandsons, Adrian and Carter.

Joan's other books include *Writing Memoir Together: A Roundtable Approach; Our Amazing New Zealand Campervan Adventure; Ireland: What We Saw, Heard, & Tasted;* and Editor of *Growing Up on Prairie Farms: A Rough & Tumble Childhood,* a pioneer memoir by Phyllis Mitchell.

www.ingramcontent.com/pod-product-compliance
Lightning Source LLC
Chambersburg PA
CBHW071000040426
42443CB00007B/598